Biography

James Egan was born in 1985 and grew up in
Portarlington, Co. Laois in the Midlands of Ireland.
In 2008, James moved to England and studied in Oxford.
James married his wife in 2012 and currently lives in
Havant in Hampshire.
James had his first book, 365 Ways to Stop Sabotaging
Your Life, published in 2014.
Several of James' books have become No.1 Best Sellers
in the UK including 1000 Facts about Horror Movies,
3000 Facts About the Greatest Movies Ever, 365 Things
People Believe That Aren't True, Another 365 Things
People Believe That Aren't True, and 500 Things People
Believe That Aren't True.

Books by James Egan

Fairytale
Inherit the Earth
Words That Need to Exist in English
Hilarious Things That Kids Say
Hilarious Things That Mums Say
3000 Facts about TV Shows
3000 Facts about Animated Shows
3000 Facts about Actors
3000 Facts about Countries
Dinosaurs Had Feathers (and other Random Facts)
3000 Facts about Animals
1000 Facts about James Bond
1000 Inspiring Facts
The Pocketbook of Phobias
How to Psychologically Survive Cancer
1000 Out-of-this-World Facts about Space
3000 Facts about the Greatest Movies Ever
1000 Facts about Film Directors
1000 Facts about Superhero Movies
1000 Facts about Superheroes Vol. 1-3
1000 Facts about Supervillains Vol. 1-3
1000 Facts about Comic Books Vol. 1-3
1000 Facts about Animated Films
1000 Facts about Horror Movies
1000 Facts about American Presidents
Adorable Animal Facts
3000 Facts about Video Games
500 Things People Believe That Aren't True
1000 Things People Believe That Aren't True
3000 Astounding Quotes
1000 Facts About Comic Book Characters Vol. 1-3
100 Classic Stories in 100 Pages
Words That Need to Exist in English
The Pocketbook of Phobias
500 Facts about Godzilla
365 Ways to Stop Sabotaging Your Life

The Biggest Movie Plotholes

by

James Egan

Copyright 2019 © James Egan

All rights reserved. No part of this book may be reproduced, stored, or transmitted by any means - whether auditory, graphic, mechanical, or electronic - without written permission of both publisher and author, except in the case of brief excerpts used in critical articles and reviews. Unauthorised reproduction of any part of this work is illegal. Unauthorised reproduction of any part of this work is illegal and is punishable by law.

ISBN: 978-0-244-77614-5

Because of the dynamic nature of the Internet, any web addresses or links contain in this book may have changed since publication and may no longer be valid. The views expressed in this work are solely those of the author and do not necessarily reflect the views of the publisher, and the publisher hereby disclaims any responsibility for them.

Any people depicted in stock imagery provided by Thinkstock are models, and such images are being used for illustrative purposes only.
Certain stock imagery © Thinkstock.

Lulu Publishing Services rev. date: 10/04/2019

Special Thanks to
X-Men: Days of Future Past

Great film but it has so many inconsistencies, it's very possible the movie was taking plothole-steroids

Introduction

When something unrealistic happens in a movie, the viewer tends to just go along with it. When the audience sacrifices realism and logic in a story for the sake of enjoyment, it is called The Suspension of Disbelief. Although plotholes are annoying, sometimes they are necessary. The best example of this is when John Wayne was promoting his film, Stagecoach, and a critic asked, "Why didn't the Indians just shoot the horses? John Wayne answered with, "If the Indians had done that, they would have stopped the picture." That's understandable. It's important for a film to be entertaining rather than realistic.

Nevertheless, it's human nature for little inconsistencies in movies to irk us. Although we know lightsabres and the Force can't exist, we accept Star Wars because we know it is simply a piece of fiction. However, there are certain parts of the story that just don't make sense. If Obi-Wan wanted to hide Luke from Darth Vader, why didn't he change Luke's name? Why did he place Luke on the same planet that Vader is from? Isn't that going to be the first place that Vader checks?

There's a part of you that can dismiss inconsistencies like this by saying, "It's only a movie!" And that's true. But still, it's really annoying when a plothole is so easy to avoid, you can't believe the scriptwriter, director, producer, or actors didn't notice. How come nobody seems to age in The Shawshank Redemption over 19 years? In Pulp Fiction, why does Mia call Vincent a "square" while outlining a rectangle? In The Nightmare Before Christmas, why does Jack Skellington ask "what's this?" when he sees snow for the first time but he calls it snow 30 seconds later?

I understand that directors are usually aware of plotholes but keep them in the film for the sake of pacing. In Jurassic Park, the ground in the T-Rex's enclosure is clearly on the same level as its cage. When the T-Rex escapes, we see that the ground is 100ft below the cage. Also, how did the T-Rex get into the visitor's centre in the final scene without anyone seeing or hearing it? How did it fit through the doors? The director, Steven Spielberg was aware of these plotholes but substituted logic for spectacle, which seemed to work out since Jurassic Park is one of the most beloved films ever.

I try to ignore plotholes like this in this book and focus on inconsistencies that are easily avoidable. So, this book is simply a bit of fun rather than a harsh critique on film itself.

But seriously, why is there a car in Braveheart? How did the continuity guy miss that?

You made a lot of mistakes, but the biggest by far is that in episode 2F09, when Itchy plays Scratchy's skeleton like a xylophone, he strikes the same rib twice in succession, yet he produces two clearly different tones. I mean, what are we to believe, that this is some sort of a magic xylophone or something? Boy, I really hope somebody got fired for that blunder.

- *Some Nerd*
(The Simpsons)

Content

1.	2001: A Space Odyssey	p16
2.	A Bug's Life	p16
3.	A Nightmare on Elm Street	p16
4.	A Quiet Place	p17
5.	Aladdin	p17
6.	Alice in Wonderland	p17
7.	Alice in Wonderland (2010)	p18
8.	Alien	p18
9.	Aliens	p19
10.	Alien^3	p19
11.	Alien: Resurrection	p20
12.	Alien: Covenant	p20
13.	Amazing Spider-Man	p21
14.	Amazing Spider-Man 2	p21
15.	Angels and Demons	p22
16.	Ant-Man	p22
17.	Ant-Man and the Wasp	p23
18.	Aquaman	p24
19.	Armageddon	p24
20.	Avatar	p25
21.	The Avengers	p25
22.	Avengers: Age of Ultron	p26
23.	Avengers: Infinity War	p27
24.	Avengers: Endgame	p27
25.	Back to the Future II	p27
26.	Batman	p29
27.	Batman Returns	p30
28.	Batman Forever	p30
29.	Batman & Robin	p31
30.	Batman Begins	p32
31.	Batman v Superman: Dawn of Justice	p33
32.	Beauty and the Beast	p33
33.	Beauty and the Beast (2017)	p34
34.	Ben-Hur	p34
35.	Big Hero 6	p34
36.	Bird Box	p35
37.	Black Panther	p36
38.	Blade	p37
39.	Bride of Frankenstein	p37
40.	Bumblebee	p38

41.	Buried	p38
42.	Captain America: The First Avenger	p38
43.	Captain America: Winter Soldier	p39
44.	Captain America: Civil War	p39
45.	Captain Marvel	p40
46.	Cars	p40
47.	Casino Royale	p40
48.	Cinderella	p41
49.	Close Encounters of the Third Kind	p41
50.	Commando	p42
51.	Conan the Barbarian	p43
52.	Daredevil	p44
53.	The Dark Knight	p45
54.	The Dark Knight Rises	p46
55.	Deadpool 2	p49
56.	Die Another Day	p49
57.	Die Hard	p50
58.	Die Hard 2: Die Harder	p50
59.	Die Hard: With A Vengeance	p51
60.	District 9	p52
61.	Django Unchained	p52
62.	Doctor Strange	p52
63.	Edward Scissorhands	p53
64.	E.T. – The Extra-Terrestrial	p53
65.	Face/Off	p53
66.	Fantastic Beasts and Where to Find Them	p54
67.	Fantastic Four	p55
68.	Fantastic Four: Rise of the Silver Surfer	p55
69.	Fant4stic	p55
70.	Fantastic Voyage	p56
71.	Fargo	p57
72.	The Fast and the Furious	p57
73.	Fast Five	p57
74.	The Fast and the Furious 6	p58
75.	The Fate of the Furious	p58
76.	The Fifth Element	p58
77.	The Fly	p59
78.	Forrest Gump	p59
79.	Friday the 13th	p60
80.	Frozen	p60
81.	Ghostbusters 2	p60
82.	Glass	p62

83.	Godzilla	p62
84.	GoldenEye	p62
85.	Goldfinger	p63
86.	The Good Dinosaur	p63
87.	Gravity	p63
88.	Green Lantern	p64
89.	Gremlins	p64
90.	Guardians of the Galaxy	p65
91.	Guardians of the Galaxy Vol. 2	p65
92.	Halloween	p65
93.	Halloween: Resurrection	p66
94.	Hancock	p66
95.	The Hangover	p66
96.	Harry Potter and the Philosopher's Stone	p67
97.	Harry Potter and the Chamber of Secrets	p68
98.	Harry Potter and the Prisoner of Azkaban	p68
99.	Harry Potter and the Goblet of Fire	p69
100.	Harry Potter and the Order of the Phoenix	p69
101.	Harry Potter and the Half-Blood Prince	p70
102.	Harry Potter and the Deathly Hallows Part 1	p70
103.	Harry Potter and the Deathly Hallows Part 2	p71
104.	Hellboy	p71
105.	Hercules	p72
106.	The Hitman's Bodyguard	p73
107.	The Hobbit: An Unexpected Journey	p73
108.	The Hobbit: Desolation of Smaug	p73
109.	The Hobbit: The Battle of Five Armies	p74
110.	Home Alone	p74
111.	Home Alone 2: Lost in New York	p75
112.	Hook	p75
113.	Ice Age	p76
114.	Ice Age: Dawn of the Dinosaurs	p76
115.	Inception	p76
116.	The Incredibles	p77
117.	The Incredibles 2	p78
118.	Independence Day	p79
119.	Indiana Jones and the Temple of Doom	p79
120.	Indiana Jones + the Kingdom of the Crystal Skull	p79
121.	Inglourious Basterds	p80
122.	Inside Out	p80
123.	Interstellar	p81
124.	Iron Man	p81

125.	Iron Man 2	p82
126.	Iron Man 3	p82
127.	IT	p83
128.	Jaws	p83
129.	Jaws IV: The Revenge	p84
130.	Jumanji	p84
131.	Jurassic Park	p85
132.	Jurassic Park: The Lost World	p85
133.	Jurassic World	p85
134.	Jurassic World: Fallen Kingdom	p86
135.	Justice League	p87
136.	The Karate Kid	p87
137.	Kick-Ass	p87
138.	Kill Bill	p88
139.	Kung Fu Panda	p88
140.	The LEGO Movie	p88
141.	The Lion King	p89
142.	The Little Mermaid	p89
143.	Logan	p90
144.	Looper	p91
145.	The Lord of the Rings: Fellowship of the Ring	p91
146.	The Lord of the Rings: The Two Towers	p92
147.	The Lord of the Rings: Return of the King	p92
148.	Man of Steel	p93
149.	The Matrix	p94
150.	The Matrix Reloaded	p95
151.	The Matrix Revolutions	p96
152.	Maximum Overdrive	p96
153.	The Meg	p97
154.	Memento	p97
155.	Men in Black	p98
156.	Men in Black III	p98
157.	Minority Report	p99
158.	Mission: Impossible	p99
159.	Mission: Impossible II	p100
160.	Mission: Impossible III	p100
161.	Mission: Impossible - Ghost Protocol	p101
162.	Mission: Impossible – Rogue Nation	p101
163.	Mission: Impossible – Fallout	p101
164.	Monsters Inc.	p102
165.	Ocean's Eleven	p102
166.	Pacific Rim	p102

167.	Paranormal Activity	p103
168.	Pirates of the Caribbean	p103
169.	Pirates of the Caribbean: Salazar's Revenge	p103
170.	Planet of the Apes (2001)	p104
171.	Pocahontas	p104
172.	Point Break	p104
173.	Poltergeist	p105
174.	Predator	p105
175.	The Princess and the Frog	p105
176.	Prometheus	p106
177.	The Purge	p107
178.	Raiders of the Lost Ark	p107
179.	Ralph Breaks the Internet	p108
180.	Ready Player One	p108
181.	Rear Window	p109
182.	Reservoir Dogs	p110
183.	The Ring	p110
184.	Rocky	p110
185.	Rocky II	p111
186.	Rocky IV	p111
187.	Rocky V	p112
188.	Rogue One	p112
189.	Saw	p113
190.	Saw II	p113
191.	Saw III	p114
192.	Scream	p114
193.	Se7en	p115
194.	The Shawshank Redemption	p115
195.	Shrek	p116
196.	Signs	p116
197.	The Simpsons Movie	p116
198.	Sinister	p116
199.	The Sixth Sense	p117`
200.	Skyfall	p118
201.	Sleeping Beauty	p119
202.	Snow White and the Seven Dwarfs	p120
203.	The Sound of Music	p120
204.	Spider-Man	p120
205.	Spider-Man 2	p121
206.	Spider-Man 3	p122
207.	Spider-Man: Homecoming	p123
208.	Split	p123

209.	Star Trek: The Motion Picture	p124
210.	Star Trek II: The Wrath of Khan	p124
211.	Star Trek	p125
212.	Star Trek: Into Darkness	p125
213.	Star Wars: Episode I – The Phantom Menace	p126
214.	Star Wars: Episode II – Attack of the Clones	p126
215.	Star Wars: Episode III – Revenge of the Sith	p127
216.	Star Wars: Episode IV – A New Hope	p127
217.	Star Wars: Episode V -The Empire Strikes Back	p127
218.	Star Wars: Episode VI - Return of the Jedi	p128
219.	Star Wars: The Force Awakens	p129
220.	Star Wars: The Last Jedi	p130
221.	Starship Troopers	p131
222.	Suicide Squad	p131
223.	Superman	p132
224.	Superman II	p132
225.	Superman III	p133
226.	Superman IV: The Quest for Peace	p133
227.	Superman Returns	p133
228.	Tangled	p134
229.	Tarzan	p134
230.	Teenage Mutant Ninja Turtles	p134
231.	Teenage Mutant Ninja Turtles II	p135
232.	Teenage Mutant Ninja Turtles (2014)	p135
233.	TMNT: Out of the Shadows	p136
234.	The Terminator	p136
235.	Terminator 2: Judgment Day	p137
236.	Terminator 3: Rise of the Machines	p138
237.	Terminator: Salvation	p138
238.	Terminator: Genisys	p138
239.	The Thing	p139
240.	Thor	p139
241.	Thor: The Dark World	p140
242.	Thor: Ragnarok	p140
243.	Thunderball	p140
244.	Titanic	p141
245.	Top Gun	p142
246.	Toy Story	p142
247.	Toy Story 2	p142
248.	Toy Story 3	p143
249.	Transformers: The Movie	p143
250.	Transformers	p143

251.	Transformers: Revenge of the Fallen	p144
252.	Transformers: Dark of the Moon	p144
253.	Transformers: Age of Extinction	p145
254.	Transformers: The Last Knight	p145
255.	Twilight	p146
256.	Twilight: New Moon	p146
257.	Twister	p146
258.	The Usual Suspects	p147
259.	V for Vendetta	p148
260.	Venom	p149
261.	The Village	p149
262.	WALL-E	p150
263.	The Wizard of Oz	p150
264.	The Wolverine	p150
265.	Wreck-It Ralph	p151
266.	X-Men	p152
267.	X2: X-Men United	p152
268.	X-Men: The Last Stand	p153
269.	X-Men Origins: Wolverine	p153
270.	X-Men: First Class	p154
271.	X-Men: Days of Future Past	p155

1. 2001: A Space Odyssey

Although the director, Stanley Kubrick has a reputation for meticulous shooting scenes over and over to make them perfect, he made a very simple error in the Moon scenes. Since the Moon has $1/6^{th}$ the gravity of Earth, the astronauts should be bouncing when they move around. In these scenes, the astronauts move normally.

2. A Bug's Life

Every season, the ants are forced to collect food to give to a group of hostile grasshoppers. The lead character, Flik accidentally knocks the food into the stream just before the grasshoppers come to the anthill. As compensation, the grasshoppers demand twice as much food the next time they come. This kickstarts the whole story as Flik desperately seeks out other bugs to help him find food for the grasshoppers.

All of this could have been avoided if the food was put ANYWHERE except beside a stream. It's like putting a bomb beside a dynamite factory. What did you expect was going to happen?

3. A Nightmare on Elm Street

To prepare for Freddy Kruger entering her house, Nancy sets up booby traps including tripwires, shotgun shells, explosives, and a sledgehammer that swings down when a specific door is opened. She sets up all these traps... in ten minutes. Personally, if a serial killer was coming to my house, I would make preparations for at least a full weekend.

4. A Quiet Place
A Quiet Place is set in a world where no one can make a noise without risking being killed by monsters that have super-hearing. Lee explains to his son, Marcus that they can speak and shout when near a waterfall because the running water drowns them out. So, why don't they live right beside it?

5. Aladdin
If Aladdin isn't allowed to touch anything in The Cave of Wonders except the lamp, how come nothing happens when he touches the magic carpet?

Also, Jafar has a sceptre that can hypnotise anyone. If he wants Jasmine to love him, why doesn't he use it on her? If he wants the lamp, why doesn't he use the sceptre to convince Aladdin to give it to him?

6. Alice in Wonderland
If there is food in Wonderland that turns people into giants, why does the Red Queen's army not

use it to enforce law? Why doesn't the people eat this food so they can overpower the Red Queen's army?

7. Alice in Wonderland (2010)

The Caterpillar shows Alice an ancient calendar that predicts the future. In the Caterpillar's exact words, "It tells of each and every day since the beginning." The calendar shows that Alice is destined to destroy the Red Queen's dragon, the Jabberwocky.

The citizens of Wonderland are terrified of the Jabberwocky since it invaded the White Queen's home, killing hundreds, including the Mad Hatter's family.

Do you know what the White Queen was doing prior to the Jabberwocky's attack? Having a party.

Why was she entertaining people when the calendar stated that her home would be incinerated by the Jabberwocky on that exact day? Why didn't the White Queen leave when she knew an attack was imminent?

8. Alien

Within an hour or so, the Xenomorph alien goes from 1ft to 8ft. It didn't eat anything so how did it become so large so quickly?

9. Aliens

The Weyland-Yutani organization seeks out the Xenomorph alien, believing they can use it as a weapon. Since Ellen Ripley is the only person alive that has had direct contact with the Xenomorph, she is asked to be an advisor for a team of marines to locate the creature. Ripley believes the marines are tasked with killing the creature and is oblivious that the organization wishes to weaponize it.

In the previous movie, the alien killed every one of Ripley's team members. There is no one who wants to see the Xenomorphs die more than her and she says they should nuke the Xenomorph's entire planet.

So why did Weyland-Yutani order Ripley to bring back a living Xenomorph when she will do everything in her power to kill it? Once they got enough intel from her, the organization should have sent Ripley away to avoid her from compromising their mission.

10. Alien^3

Although Ripley defeated the Xenomorph Queen in the conclusion of the previous film, the beginning of Alien^3 shows that it managed to lay an egg on the ship. A facehugger hatched from the egg and laid another egg inside Ripley while she was in cryosleep.

However, there doesn't seem to be a point where the Queen could have laid the egg.

Also, the facehugger broke through Ripley's cryochamber using its acidic blood.

How did the acid not melt Ripley's face? How did it not malfunction the cryochamber?

How could the facehugger implant its egg in Ripley while she was in cryosleep? Wouldn't Ripley have noticed something was wrong with her chamber immediately after waking?

11.   Alien: Resurrection

Ripley's clone has acid blood like the Xenomorphs since she was made from their DNA. In several scenes, we see her blood melting metal upon contact.

So how are the doctors able to perform surgery on her in the opening scene without the procedure melting the surgical tools?

12.   Alien: Covenant

Alien: Covenant is the sequel to Prometheus. Viewers criticised the previous film due to scenes showing highly-trained astronauts casually taking off their helmets on an extra-terrestrial planet. No scientist in their right mind would attempt this (even if the air was supposedly breathable) since they would be exposed to poisonous fumes or bacteria.

Sadly, the director ignored this criticism and so, the crew do the exact same thing in this film. Unsurprisingly, viewers once again commented on how idiotic this action is.

This sort of behaviour contradicts the characters of the original movie who were terrified of bringing an alien onboard since it could infect the ship with bacteria or germs.

13.   Amazing Spider-Man

After Doctor Curt Connors lost his arm, he used a lizard's regenerating properties to create a concoction that will regrow his limb. However, the reptile's DNA turns Connors into a monster called The Lizard. Although he feels invincible in this form, he returns to normal after a few hours and must inject himself with the concoction again to become The Lizard once more. Connors wants everyone to feel as strong as he does so he plans to turn everyone in the city into lizards.

But there's one part of this plan that nobody addresses. If Connors achieves his plan, everyone will turn into lizards... and then just turn back to normal after a few hours. So, what is Connor's long-term goal?

14.   Amazing Spider-Man 2

When Max Dillon gets electrocuted by eels, he gains the ability to control electricity and becomes the supervillain, Electro. This accident also fixes the gap in Dillon's teeth. I'm not kidding. The camera literally zooms in on Dillon's teeth to show that the... electricity has corrected his toothgap. What does this have to do with anything??

15. Angels and Demons

This film has a plothole that is very common in stories where a villain devises a scheme that is impossible to plan. Dr. Langton is tasked with finding an anti-matter bomb in the Vatican before it explodes. With the help of The Camerlengo, Langton succeeds.

We learn soon after that The Camerlengo was the mastermind behind this plot.

However, he tried to kill Langton earlier in the Vatican Library. Why would The Camerlengo try and kill him when he needed Langton to find the bomb?

16. Ant-Man

Let's say that Ant-Man weighs 180lbs. When he shrinks to the size of an ant, he should still weight 180lbs. The space between his atoms have shrunk but he has the same mass, meaning that it should be impossible for him to perform feats like run on a gun barrel or jump on a person's shoulder as is depicted in the film.

Also, Hank Pym tells Scott Lang the shrinking technology is only possible by using Pym Particles. However, overexposure to these particles causes a person to become mentally unstable.

When Darren Cross threatens to kill Scott's friends, Hank warns Cross that he has gone insane because the Pym Particles are interfering with his mind. This is impossible because Cross hasn't figured out how to use the Pym Particles. He is trying to kill Hank and Scott BECAUSE he can't duplicate the Pym Particles.

17. Ant-Man and the Wasp

When Ant-Man sees that Wasp's suit has wings, he says to the inventor, Hank Pym, "You gave her wings? So, I take it you didn't have that tech available for me?" Hank replies by saying, "No, I did."

Although this is a funny line, it creates a plothole. When Ant-Man shrinks, he relies on getting around by hitchhiking on an ant. Sometimes, Ant-Man can't locate an ant, so he risks not getting to his destination in time.

What if Ant-Man needed to deactivate a bomb but couldn't locate an ant? Imagine if the bomb detonated, killing dozens of people even though it could have been stopped if Ant-Man had wings but Pym chose not to attach them to his suit.

18. Aquaman

The Atlantean king, Orm the Ocean Master wishes to declare war on the surface world since humans have polluted the oceans with trash. Orm sends this trash back to the surface as a warning to humanity.

If he has the power to do this, why doesn't he and the rest of the Atlanteans just send garbage to the surface all the time? Humanity have been dumping a huge amount of trash in the ocean for the past century. The pollution in the ocean is killing all forms of marine life. Why did it take so long for the Atlanteans to retaliate?

Also, there is a scene where Pteranodons are in the Earth's core. That is also a bit unrealistic.

19. Armageddon

NASA learns that an asteroid is about to collide with Earth, killing all life on the planet. The organization sends professional drillers into space to drill a bomb into the asteroid and then detonate it.

However, training to go into space is so intense, it would make more sense to train astronauts how to drill. Ben Affleck, who plays AJ in the film, pointed out this plothole to the director, Michael Bay. Bay told Affleck to "shut the &*%^ up." Which he did.

20. Avatar

When the RDA decide to bomb the Na'vi's hometree, Michelle Rodriguez's character, Trudy refuses to take part and flies away.

Despite violating a direct order, Trudy suffers no consequences. If a soldier refuses a direct order, they can be removed from their position or jailed.

Also, Trudy isn't in a normal war. If the humans lose, they go extinct. Despite the fact her actions risked the end of her species, she suffers no consequences. She doesn't even get told off!

21. The Avengers

We learn in later movies that the reason why Thanos wants the Tesseract is because it houses the Space Stone, which is one of six Infinity Stones he needs to complete his Infinity Gauntlet.

In this film, he tasks Loki with retrieving the Tesseract. To help him overpower the forces of Earth, Thanos gives Loki a mind-controlling weapon called The Sceptre. The Sceptre is powered by another one of the Infinity Stones, the Mind Stone.

Wait... if Thanos desperately covets the six Infinity Stones, why does he give one so freely to Loki to retrieve another one?

Also, how do all The Avengers speak to each in the final battle when they are clearly not wearing ear pieces? Do they all have really, really, REALLY good hearing?

22. Avengers: Age of Ultron

It seems kind of redundant to point out that a film with gods and robots is unrealistic but I have to when the plothole is so easy to avoid. Iron Man 3 concludes with Tony Stark having his arc reactor removed from his chest. The reactor allows Tony to pilot the Iron Man suit.

What's he doing in the first scene in this film? Piloting the Iron Man suit.

Obviously, we knew Tony Stark wouldn't quit as a superhero. He's basically the face of the Marvel Cinematic Universe.

So why show a scene of him removing the arc reactor, symbolising that Tony's retiring as a superhero when he isn't? It utterly defeats the ending of Iron Man 3.

This could be fixed with a single line of dialogue. Tony could have casually mentioned that he figured out how to get the suit working without relying on an arc reactor fused into his chest.

Also, Ultron keeps referring to the meteor that killed off the dinosaurs. The dinosaurs were killed by an asteroid, not a meteor. I bet this line really irked astronomers.

23. Avengers: Infinity War

Thanos seeks out the Infinity Stones, which will give him the power to wipe out half the universe with a snap of his fingers. His step-daughter, Gamora, is the only person in the universe that knows the location of one of the stones, the Soul Stone.

So, what does Gamora do? She flies straight to Thanos! She could have sent any of her teammates to fight him but instead, Gamora goes herself. Why didn't she go… anywhere else in the universe?

24. Avengers: Endgame

In Avengers: Infinity War, Groot used part of his body to create a hilt for Thor's hammer, Stormbreaker.

Later, Thanos uses the Infinity Gauntlet to wipe out half of all life in the universe, including Groot. If this is the case, Stormbreaker's hilt should have disappeared at the same time that Groot died.

25. Back to the Future II

There is an inconsistency that many people have pointed out with the first Back to the Future movie. Marty goes back in time and meets his parents. When he returns to his normal time, his parents never point out that Marty looks remarkably like that guy they met when they were in high school.

Personally, I've never had a problem with this plothole. During that time period, they only met Marty for a couple of days and didn't see him at that age for over 20 years. They're not going to look at him and say, "Hey! You look like that guy from two decades ago! Clearly, you are a time-traveller!"

However, there is another plothole that opens up a bigger can of worms. In Back to the Future II, Marty falls from Biff's building, seemingly plummeting to his death. However, Doc Brown flew his DeLorean just below Marty, easily catching him.

When Marty goes back in time and is chased in a tunnel by Biff, Doc Brown saves him by dropping a rope for Marty to grab onto.

Both of these situations have the same plothole. How did Doc Brown know the exact place and time to rescue Marty? Both times, he didn't know Marty was in trouble. The only way this is possible… is if Marty already died.

Think about it. If Doc Brown didn't rescue Marty in that tunnel, Marty would have been run down by Biff.

Doc would have found out about Marty's death shortly after (probably from the news,) and so, could go back in time to just before Marty's death to rescue him.

Marty may have died many times throughout the Back to the Future trilogy but Doc keeps reversing it with time-travel.

You might think – That's not a plothole. In fact, it fixes a plothole. Unfortunately, this creates a plothole, not just in Back to the Future but every movie that has time-travel. Once time-travel is involved in a story, there can't really be any tension or urgency because YOU CAN LITERALLY CONTROL TIME! No matter how many times Doc fails, he can just go back in time and try again.

In many stories, characters seem to forget that time-travel is a thing or choose not to use it when it's incredibly convenient. This is a problem with other time-travel movies like The Terminator and Harry Potter and the Prisoner of Azkaban.

26. Batman

Although this film is top-notch, there are plotholes galore in the final scene. While piloting his Batwing, Batman shoots at the Joker with machine guns and missiles. How does he miss?

You literally see the Joker in the dead-centre of the Batwing's radar.

Also, while Batman is firing at him, the Joker just stands there without a care in the world. Did he know Batman would miss?

The Joker then blows up the Batwing with a gun. Despite the fact you see the vehicle explode, Batman is able to escape with mild injuries. Why wasn't he incinerated?

The Joker then kidnaps Vicki Vale and runs into a large building. As Batman ascends the building, he is met with numerous henchmen, which he is forced to battle. Why were the henchmen in that building? The Joker decided at the last second to go in there. Does the Joker have goons randomly hiding in every building in his proximity? Even the director, Tim Burton, couldn't explain this.

27. Batman Returns
How come nobody can figure out that Bruce Wayne is Batman considering he has a Bat-Signal on the roof of his house?

28. Batman Forever
At Edward Nygma's business party, he shows off his brainwave device which reveals the user's greatest desire on a huge monitor. After being

coaxed by Nygma, Bruce Wayne agrees to use the device.

Why would Bruce Wayne allow a machine to look into his mind, knowing it can easily reveal his secret identity as Batman?

Also, Bruce has already seen that the device will show what he is thinking on a massive monitor which hundreds of people can see. If it showed a picture of Batman, he would have been screwed.

29. Batman & Robin

There are so many inconsistencies in Batman & Robin, you could write a whole book about it and it would be longer than the screenplay.

However, the biggest problem is probably the villains' plan. Mister Freeze wants to create a global Ice Age. Poison Ivy wants plants to cover the entire world.

So, how are plants going to thrive in sub-zero temperature? Why don't the villains point out that their goals conflict with each other? If you paid me, I wouldn't be able to think of two of Batman's supervillains who's interests conflict with each other more than Ivy and Freeze.

Also, if Freeze needs to stay cold to live, why does he wear fuzzy slippers and a dressing gown? Why does he smoke cigars? Is this film allergic to making sense?

30. Batman Begins

When Bruce Wayne completes his training with Ra's Al Ghul, he is asked to show his commitment by executing a criminal. Bruce Wayne states that he does not believe in murder and so, the criminal must be judged in a court of law. When Ra's disagrees with him, Bruce blows up Ra's temple, killing dozens of people! That is a tad hypocritical.

Also, Batman regularly uses a sonic weapon, causing thousands of bats fly to his destination. Despite this incredibly handy gadget, he never uses it in the sequels.

Probably the biggest plothole that viewers fixate on is the villain's scheme. Ra's Al Ghul has filtered a Fear Toxin into the Gotham water supply. Touching or drinking this water has no effect on a person since the toxin only works when the liquid evaporates.

When the villain activates a microwave emitter, which vaporizes all the water in the city, it triggers the Fear Toxin, causing everyone in Gotham to hallucinate.

Many people have pointed out that the microwave emitter should have killed everyone in Gotham because human beings are composed of 71% water.

However, that inconsistency doesn't bother me. I always assumed the machine only vaporizes water in its pure state.

However, there's another inconsistency I have a problem with. The Scarecrow mentions that the Fear Toxin has been inserted into the water supply for months. Are you telling me that not one person in Gotham boiled a kettle in all that time?

31.   Batman v Superman: Dawn of Justice
Batman has a vision that the world will be consumed by Darkseid's forces and Superman will become evil. He then wakes up to see the Flash has travelled from the future to the present to warn Bruce Wayne that "Lois is the key." Bruce Wayne then wakes up... again.

How is Bruce Wayne suddenly able to see into the future? He didn't just have a premonition. He had a premonition inside another dream. Is this Inception?

Also, did the Flash travel through time AND inside Bruce Wayne's dream? How did the director read this scene in the script and say, "Yup, that makes sense."

32.   Beauty and the Beast
Lumiere tells Belle that the inhabitants of the castle have been cursed for ten years.

However, Chip is clearly younger than ten. So how does that work? Do I want to know?

Also, the narrator says that curse will be broken if the Prince finds love before his 21st year. This means that the Prince was turned into a Beast when he was 11.

However, the painting of the Prince seen at the beginning clearly shows him as a young man.

33.   Beauty and the Beast (2017)
The Beast shows Belle a magical book that can transport the reader to anywhere they desire.

When Belle learns her father is ill, Beast tells her to go find him. Belle leaves the castle to rescue her father and bring him home. Why didn't she use the book to teleport to her father's position?

34.   Ben-Hur
A car appears for a second during the chariot scene. This film is set in 28AD… Do I have to say anything else?

35.   Big Hero 6
To enrol in a school science fair, Hiro presents his project – microbots. This swarm of little robots can combine to form into any shape the wielder desires.

The biggest tech company, Krei Tech, wants to market the microbots, showing Hiro that his invention is worth a fortune. Sadly, a fire destroys the school, killing Hiro's brother, Tadashi.

Hiro learns that his microbots were not destroyed in the blast and a mysterious being called The Phantom is using them for his own desires.

Despite the fact Hiro desperately tries to retrieve his microbots, he never considers just... making them again. Hiro is the one who invented them. If Hiro wants them back, why doesn't he just make more?

36. Bird Box

The story revolves around a group of unseen monsters that invade society. Anyone who makes eye contact with these monsters is driven irreversibly suicidal.

Malorie and a group of survivors leave their safehouse to find food at a local supermarket. When they get there, they see a cage of birds and notice the birds go crazy when the monsters are nearby. This convinces Malorie to keep the birds with them at all times. They then head back to the safehouse.

First off, why are there live birds in a supermarket? Why aren't they in a pet store?

Secondly, how are the birds going to help? The characters keep their eyes closed or wear blindfolds to ensure they won't see the monsters. It's not like they say, "Oh, the bird is chirping. I better close my eyes" since their eyes ARE ALREADY CLOSED!

Thirdly, why doesn't Malorie and the gang just stay at the supermarket? They went there in the first place because they were running out of food.

This isn't just an oversight from the writer. John Malkovich's character, Douglas points out they should stay at the supermarket since they could live off the food for months.

But the characters just... don't... for no reason. Obviously, they have to head back to the safehouse to give the food to the rest of the survivors but there's nothing to stop them from heading back to the supermarket

37. Black Panther

Black Panther's nation of Wakanda is the most technologically advanced nation on Earth. It is the only country that has never been invaded nor has it invaded another.

They refuse to share their vibranium technology with the rest of society, afraid that people will repurpose it for war. Of course,

Wakanda would never misuse vibranium as the nation is above barbarism.

And how do the Wakandans elect a leader? With a battle to the death. How could the country emphasise how they must maintain peace for millennia while electing their ruler in the most primitive way possible?

38. Blade

The vampire hunter, Blade impales and incinerates the vampire, Quinn. Although Quinn is charred to a crisp, he survives since he is a vampire.

When he is being dissected at the hospital, Quinn wakes up and kills one of the doctors. As he is about to kill another doctor, Blade arrives to kill Quinn.

If he knew Quinn was alive, why didn't Blade kill him in their first encounter? Blade is a vampire hunter so he knew burning Quinn wouldn't kill him. So why let him live if Blade was only going to kill Quinn later that same day?

39. Bride of the Frankenstein

Although Maria's father is called Ludwig, his name was Hans in the previous film and he was played by a different actor. This is extra confusing since you see the original actor in the prologue.

40. Bumblebee

Although the film is set in 1987, we regularly see technology that didn't exist back then. Shatter shows a hologram of the International Space Station in Earth's orbit despite the fact the ISS wasn't launched until 1998.

Touchscreens are displayed on the communications tower even though they didn't exist back then.

Also, the agents M4 guns weren't produced until 1993.

I don't think transforming robots existed back then either.

41. Buried

Ryan Reynold's character, Paul wakes up inside a buried coffin. Paul has a Blackberry which he uses to ring people to help find his position so he can escape before he runs out of air.

At no point does Paul simply use Google Maps and GPS to find out where he is and give his exact location to his rescuers.

42. Captain America: The First Avenger

Immediately after Bucky Barnes seemingly dies when he falls from a train, Captain America captures the evil scientist, Arnim Zola. Zola is seen immediately after being interrogated by Colonel Philips.

We learn in the sequel that Bucky survived the fall and was brainwashed by Arnim Zola to become a sleeper agent. How could Zola do this if he was arrested seconds after Bucky fell off the train?

43. Captain America: Winter Soldier

The film reveals that thousands of members from the terrorist group, Hydra infiltrated the counter-terrorist organization, SHIELD over the last few years. Nobody knew about this... which is weird since Tony Stark hacked into SHIELD during the events in The Avengers and didn't notice that Hydra was preparing to kill hundreds of thousands of civilians.

Later, Black Widow infiltrates Alexander Pierce's World Security Council by using hologram technology to disguise her face. Although many of the characters have been on the run for most of the film, Black Widow only decided to use this tech one time. Even though she and many other Avengers are on the run in the sequel, she never uses this tech again.

44. Captain America: Civil War

After Thaddeus Ross informs The Avengers that a bill will be signed that will ensure that superheroes must work with the government or face jail time, it splits the team in half. Tony Stark's arrogance led to the creation of Ultron, which nearly destroyed the world so he see the registration as a perfect opportunity to stop reckless acts like that happening ever again.

So, what does Tony do to prove this? He hires a 15-year-old Spider-Man to fight with him against a wanted criminal, a flying witch, an archer, a winged soldier, and a suspected brainwashed terrorist.

45. Captain Marvel
When Captain Marvel meets Nick Fury in 1994, he informs her that he is a SHIELD agent.

But in the film, Iron Man, Nick Fury's partner, Agent Coulson said the organization wasn't called SHIELD until 2008.

46. Cars
Nobody drives cars in this world. So why does every vehicle have doors?

47. Casino Royale
James Bond kills a man by shooting him through the eye with a nail gun.

Nail guns don't shoot nails like a normal firearm. They only discharge nails if pressed against a hard, flat surface. This plothole applies to any film where a nail gun is used like a regular gun e.g. Lethal Weapon 2, Final Destination 3, etc. If nail guns fired nails like this, they'd be almost as effective as normal guns.

48. Cinderella

Cinderella's fairy godmother uses her magic to turn the titular character's rags into a beautiful dress. She turns a pumpkin into a carriage, mice into horses, a dog into a servant, and Cinderella's shoes into glass slippers.

At the stroke of midnight, the magic spell wears off and everything reverts to normal... except the glass slippers. If the glass slippers returned to normal, the prince would have never discovered the identity of Cinderella so this inconsistency is necessary for the sake of the plot but it's still worth mentioning.

49. Close Encounters of the Third Kind

After Roy witnesses a UFO, he becomes so obsessed with aliens, he loses his job and abandons his family.

Through the extra-terrestrials' influence, Roy and hundreds of other people head to Devil's Tower to witness a UFO landing. An alien steps out of his flying saucer with dozens of people who have been abducted over the years. The alien takes Roy into the UFO, which then flies into space.

This is supposed to be an uplifting ending (I think,) but it raises many questions. Roy abandoned his entire life to see this UFO, which means it's likely that the hundreds of other people who made their way to Devil's Tower did the same thing. Like Roy, they probably quit their job, left their kids, or at the very least, have a reputation for being crazy.

That's not a far-fetched idea since Roy meets a woman on the way to Devil's Tower who is hysterical after the aliens abducted her son.

Although she is reunited with her son, what about the people who had been abducted for over 30 years? How are they supposed to have a normal life? How are all these people expected to return home after they voluntarily left their families?

Although the alien seems to have done all this for the greater good, he is actually a pretty big jerk if you think about it.

50. Commando

Okay, this is one of the most ridiculous action films ever. Arnold Schwarzenegger's character, John Matrix gets shot at by 72 people (I counted) and doesn't get hit once. Although it's highly improbable that he could survive such an assault, it's not impossible.

You know what is impossible? Surviving a 75ft fall from a plane which is travelling 180mph. You might think that since Matrix landed in water, it should cushion the impact. However, the water is only 1ft deep. Even if it was 10ft deep, hitting water at that speed and velocity would have the same impact as landing on concrete.

This plothole applies to any film where a character falls a huge distance and survives because they landed in water e.g. Predator, The Fugitive.

51. Conan the Barbarian

The most iconic sword-forging scene in movie history is from Conan the Barbarian. Most films show the sword-forging process the same way – the metal is heated before being bash it into the shape of a sword. When the blade cools, the sword is ready.

Forging swords isn't that easy. Making one sword takes at least 40 hours but it can take over three days.

And that's just the blade. That's not including the handle, the guard, or the pommel. Forging a single dagger can take 50 hours.

52. Daredevil

After a criminal is killed at a train station, the reporter, Ben Urich asks a cop if they can confirm if Daredevil was responsible. When the cop says there is no evidence that Daredevil was involved, Ben flicks his cigarette at the ground, which lands on gasoline. The gasoline lights up, creating Daredevil's symbol, proving he was there.

Although this is a cool reveal, it makes no sense if you overanalyse it (which I do.) After Daredevil killed the criminal, he got gasoline and poured it on the ground to make his symbol. Where did he get the gasoline from? Did he have it ready? Did he go to the shop and came back to the train station to make his mark?

What if nobody noticed the gasoline on the ground? That would mean Daredevil went through all that for nothing.

What if someone slipped on the gasoline? That could get someone killed!

What if the gasoline was lit by a dropped cigarette while the train station was filled with people? Daredevil could have been responsible for dozens of people being set on fire.

Also, how did Ben know the gasoline was there? If he could smell it, how come nobody else could?

Did Ben know there was gasoline there and he thought himself, "This cop doesn't believe Daredevil was here. I bet that gasoline is the same shape as Daredevil's symbol. I know what to do. I am going to flick my cigarette at it, revealing the symbol to the police to make them look stupid."

If that's the case, I'm pretty sure Daredevil is psychic.

53. The Dark Knight

Despite the fact The Dark Knight is often perceived as the greatest superhero film ever, it has a lot of glaring plotholes from the very first scene. Before the Joker is about to be shot by one the bank robbers, a bus crashes into him. How did the Joker know that the bus would hit the criminal at that exact moment? What if the criminal shot the Joker a second earlier?

The Joker then escapes the bank in the same bus. Since the bus is completely covered in dust and rubble, it's going to be pretty easy for the police to locate it.

Later, the Joker crashes Bruce Wayne's party with a group of henchmen, each armed with guns. When the Joker hurls Rachel out of a window, Batman jumps out of the building and catches her.

Some people criticise this scene, saying that they should have died when they hit the ground. However, you can clearly see Batman's cape slowing down their descent, which softens their fall.

However, the Joker is now in a room armed to the teeth with a hundred guests.

What happened? Did he kill them? It's never mentioned again.

This is actually explained in a deleted scene but I don't like the idea of a plothole being clarified in a scene that didn't make it into the final cut.

Later, it is revealed that an Wayne Enterprises employee called Coleman has abductively reasoned that Bruce Wayne is Batman. When Coleman is about to divulge this information on live-television, the Joker stops him by putting a bounty on his head.

The Dark Knight Rises takes place eight years later... In those eight years, did anyone think of asking Coleman who Batman is? I'm pretty sure not revealing the identity of a vigilante and suspected killer is a felony.

54. The Dark Knight Rises

The film begins with Bane destroying a plane but making it look like it accidentally crashed. How does he stage the plane crash as an accident? By shooting hundreds upon hundreds of bullets into the plane. I'm sure that'll fool the cops.

When John Blake meets Bruce Wayne for the first time, he feels like Bruce's persona is a pretence to mask his anger.

Based on this, Blake deduces that Bruce Wayne is Batman. How did he draw that conclusion? Based on what? He had no evidence! You're telling me that Blake figured out that Bruce was a masked vigilante because he is good at hiding his emotions?

Anyway, Blake's confrontation with him convinces Bruce to become Batman again.

However, his doctor points out that Bruce's knee cartilage has eroded. Bruce counters this by getting leg braces, giving him superstrength... which are never referenced again.

Bane enters The Stock Exchange and makes false transactions by using Bruce Wayne's fingerprints, which leaves Bruce bankrupt. However, everyone at the bank witnessed that it was Bane who made the transaction, not Bruce. Because of this, Bruce wouldn't be shut off from his accounts. Instead, he would be reimbursed.

During a fight, Bane breaks Batman's back. Instead of killing him, he flies Batman to India and imprisons him in the same jail that Bane was trapped in many years ago. I'm not sure why Bane flies with him as it would take over a day to fly to India and back to America. Bane could have sent anyone with Bruce… or just kill him. It's way easier.

When the Gotham police force believe Bane is hiding in the city's sewers, they send all the cops down there. Bane detonates bombs in the sewers, trapping the police under the city.

However, Bane could have been stopped if the police force didn't send EVERY SINGLE COP in the city under the sewer. That's like 50,000 police officers! About a hundred soldiers were sent on the manhunt against Osama Bin Laden! Why do you need 50,000 cops to find one guy? That's a bit excessive.

Also, why don't the police just escape the sewers through manholes? You would think one of them would have figured that out since they are trapped in the sewers for six months.

After Bruce Wayne's back heals from the doctor's remedy of spine-punching, he escapes prison. However, it's never explained how he gets back to Gotham.

Also, before Bruce returns, he is aware that Bane plans to destroy Gotham. So, what is the first thing Batman does when gets back?

He creates a huge Bat insignia out of fire. That must have taken ages! How is that a priority when the whole city is going to explode in a few hours?

At the end of the film, Bruce Wayne seems to sacrifice his life to save Gotham. In the final scene, Alfred is having a coffee at a café in Florence when he sees Bruce Wayne, proving that he faked his death so he can spend the rest of his life with his lover, Selina Kyle.

However, Bruce Wayne has a reputation as a playboy billionaire. All it would take is one photograph of Bruce Wayne for him to be publicly exposed. He's not even wearing a disguise! Wear a fake nose or shave your head or something.

Also, if Bruce wants to retire somewhere where no one will find him, maybe he shouldn't go to Florence; a city with nearly 400,000 people.

55. Deadpool 2

After Russell kills Cable's family, Cable goes back in time to kill him when Russell was a teenager.

After tracking Russell in a prison, Deadpool knocks Cable out of the building before plummeting into the water below.

After that, Cable leaves for no reason. Why didn't he go back inside the prison to kill Russell?

56. Die Another Day

Gustav Graves is revealed to be the villain in the opening scene, Tan-Sun. Although Tan-Sun is

Korean, he went through gene therapy to make him come across as Caucasian.

When Gustav Graves first appears, 13 months have passed since Tan-Sun's apparent demise and he already has a reputation as a billionaire philanthropist and has received a knighthood.

How could Tan-Sun do all this in just over a year while converting into a Caucasian?

57. Die Hard

There is a plothole that has appeared in countless action movies but I'm going to use Die Hard as an example as it is one of the most iconic action films.

Although Gruber is a criminal, he convinces John McClane that he is a hostage in a terrorist attack. McClane seems to trust him and gives Gruber a gun. Gruber reveals he is responsible for the terrorist attack and fires the gun at McClane, only to learn that the weapon has no bullets. However, a fully-loaded handgun is noticeably heavier than a gun with an empty clip. Bullets are made of metal. Metal is heavy. In real life, a person can easily tell if a gun has bullets or not.

58. Die Hard 2: Die Harder

Colonel Stuart hacks an airport's control system, which leaves every aircraft in the area unable to communicate, leading to one of the planes crashing. If an airplane couldn't communicate with its designated flight controller, it would simply seek out another one through its radio so it could land somewhere else.

The plane in this film is forced to land in the airport that the terrorists have taken over due to an intense heavy snow.

However, the terrorists could not have factored the blizzard into their plan. If it didn't snow, their plan would have failed spectacularly.

59. Die Hard: With A Vengeance

The terrorist, Simon taunts John McClane with riddles. If McClane solves a riddle, he will receive a clue to stop Simon's next terrorist act.

Halfway through the film, McClane believes that Simon planted a bomb in a school named after the 21st president.

However, McClane doesn't know who the 21st US president is, which causes him to frantically try and find the right school.

Although this film was made in the 1990s before a person could easily look up the information online, why doesn't McClane just run into a library and find a history book to learn the identity of this president? (In case you were wondering, the 21st US president was Chester A. Arthur.)

60. District 9

In 1982, a million aliens called Prawns landed in Johannesburg in their spaceship. After many years, the aliens were forced to live in a slum, putting up with abuse and violence from locals. They desperately looked for a way to synthesise fuel for their ship so they can go home.

In 2010, a weapons manufacturer company called MNU decided to relocate the Prawns on the exact same day the aliens manage to synthesis their fuel. What are the odds of that?

Also, the man in charge of this relocation, Wikus, accidentally sprays himself with some of this fuel, which gradually turns him into a Prawn.

Although this plot device is done for the sake of the story so Wikus can relate with the Prawns and eventually ally with them, it doesn't make any sense. Why would fuel turn a human into one of these aliens?

61. Django Unchained

Dynamite is used in many scenes throughout the film despite the fact it wasn't invented until six years after the story is based.

62. Doctor Strange

The villain, Kaecilius needs to perform a ritual to open The Dark Dimension to release his master,

Dormammu. He steals some pages from an ancient book in the library of Kamar-Taj that tells him how to open this portal. When the sorcerers of Kamar-Taj and Doctor Strange see which pages that Kaecilius has torn out, they realise what he about to do.

However, there is no way anyone would have figured out Kaecilius' plan if he just... stole the whole book.

Also, Doctor Strange uses the exact same book to learn how to use the spells needed to defeat Kaecilius. If the evil sorceror took the whole book, Strange would have never stood a chance against him.

63.   Edward Scissorhands
How does Edward drag blocks of ice into his attic? Where did he find them? Did he order them online?

64.   E.T. – The Extra-Terrestrial
After government agents stumble upon a group of E.T's, the aliens flee in their spaceship, leaving one behind. Later, we learn E.T. can fly. So why didn't he just fly up to his spaceship earlier?

65.   Face/Off
FBI agent, Sean Archer injures the terrorist, Castor Troy, leaving him in a coma. When the FBI

learns that Troy activated a bomb that will detonate in the city in a few days, they try to cut a deal with Castor's brother, Pollux but he refuses to play ball.

Desperate, Sean has a surgical procedure where he swaps faces with Castor and pretends to be him so he can learn the bomb's location from Pollux. The surgeons say the plan should work since Castor and Sean are the same height and build.

This is completely implausible. A face transplant isn't going to change Sean's hairline, jaw shape, bone structure, and skin complexion.

66. Fantastic Beasts and Where to Find Them

Just before a magizoologist called Newt Scamander arrives in New York, an inspector checks his suitcase. Although the suitcase houses dozens of magical creatures, Newt activates a switch before presenting it to the inspector so its contents seem normal.

Why doesn't Newt have the suitcase pre-emptively adjusted to this setting? Why doesn't he always have the suitcase to this setting just in case a normal human opens it? Why only activate this switch seconds before the inspector has to open it?

67.   Fantastic Four
When Johnny Storm goes "supernova" in the titanium chamber, his sister, Susan tells him that he reached a temperature of 4000 degrees Celsius, which is "the temperature of the Sun." Firstly, titanium melts at just under 2,000 degrees and boils at around 3,500 degrees.

Secondly, saying the Sun is 4,000 degrees doesn't make sense. The Sun's temperature varies tremendously. The coldest parts of it is 6,000 degrees (which is 2,000 degrees off Susan's estimate,) and the hottest part is 15 million degrees which is waaaaaaaaay off Susan's calculations. Considering Susan is one of the world's smartest scientists, you'd think she would know that.

68.   Fantastic Four: Rise of the Silver Surfer
After being exposed to cosmic radiation, Reed Richards gained the ability to stretch his body to a phenomenal level. But how does his clothes stretch without tearing?

69.   Fant4stic
Reed Richards' team successfully figure out how to send a transport pod to another dimension. The team's overseer, Dr. Allen leaves to find volunteers for the expedition to this dimension.

Since Reed's team built the machine, they feel like they deserve to be the first people to enter the new dimension. As a result, they use the pod without Dr. Allen's knowledge.

Now, you might ask - How did Dr. Allen not know Reed was doing this? Because the facility that contained this teleportation device did not have one single guard. There's no guards on the outside of the building either. There are no guards in the same room as the teleporter, despite the fact it is the most significant scientific breakthrough in history.

In fact, Reed is able to invite his friend, Ben into facility without any effort. The average bank has more security than this building.

70. Fantastic Voyage

This film isn't as well-known as the majority of films on this list but I had to include it as it is one of the biggest plotholes in movie history.

Jan Renes is a scientist who invented a shrinking ray. After he develops a blood clot in his brain, a team decide to shrink themselves to go inside him and destroy the clot. The team enter a submarine, which is then shrunk to microscopic size before being inserted into Renes. The group have a time limit to destroy the clot because they will eventually grow back to normal size.

Although the submarine is irreparably damaged, the group manage to destroy the clot and escape Renes' body before they grow to normal size.

However, the submarine is still inside Renes body and it is never explained why it doesn't grow back to normal size.

71. Fargo

The most iconic scene in Fargo is when Gaear kills his partner, Carl and disposes of his body in a woodchipper. Instead of hiding Carl's body, Gaear thought it would make more sense to grind his body into a chipper, causing gallons of blood to spew all over the ground.

Also, Gaear does this in the snow, making all of the blood stand out WAY more. How did Gaear think he wasn't going to get caught?

72. The Fast and the Furious

In all The Fast and the Furious movies, the drivers keep shifting gears at an impossible rate. In the first film, Dom and Brian shift gears eight times while racing.

73. Fast Five

In the climax, Dom and his crew tear a ten-ton vault out of a police station using their cars, dragging it through the city.

How does Dom's car not flip over every time he turns if the vault weighs ten tons? That's simple physics (which The Fast and the Furious franchise isn't a big fan of.)

Also, how does Dom drive around the city while smashing through buildings with a colossal vault dragging behind him without killing a single person?

74. The Fast and the Furious 6
The airplane drives down the runway for 13 minutes, meaning that would have to be at least 28 miles long. The longest runway in the world is just over three miles long.

75. The Fate of the Furious
When Dom looks like he is about to be killed by an explosion, his friends use their cars to shield him from the blast. Just to let you know, you can't deflect an explosion with cars and love.

76. The Fifth Element
Leeloo is The Supreme Being, meaning that it is her destiny to save humanity. Shortly after she develops consciousness, Leeloo learns every word in alphabetical order.

When she reaches the letter W, Leeloo learns about the concept of war and becomes so disillusioned, she refuses to help humanity.

How did she not learn about war earlier? Surely, she would have learned about it by studying words like genocide, murder, gun, battle, missile, tank, extermination, etc. Leeloo should have learned about the concept of war at the letter "a" when she learned what an atomic bomb was.

Also, Leeloo is considered to be The Fifth Element. However, anyone who has studied a Periodic Table will tell you that the fifth element is Boron.

77. The Fly

The scientist, Seth Brundle uses a teleportation device to transport from one pod to another. Not realising that a fly has snuck into his pod, his DNA fuses with the insect when he teleports. This causes Brundle to gradually turn into a fly hybrid.

However, the human body is covered in mites, parasites, and over a trillion types of bacteria. Why doesn't Brundle fuse with them?

78. Forrest Gump

How come nobody seems to recognise Forrest considering he is famous in almost every field – war, sports, business, indirectly bringing down President Richard Nixon, etc.

79. Friday the 13th

When Brenda is thrown out of the window by the killer, Alice runs outside to see Mrs. Voorhees pull up in her jeep.

We find out minutes later that Mrs. Voorhees is the killer. How could she have thrown Brenda out of the window if she pulled up to the location seconds later?

80. Frozen

Elsa can create ice. That's a pretty big deal. You know what's a bigger deal? She created a sentient snowman called Olaf.

Creating ice is nowhere near as important as CREATING LIFE! Is Elsa a god? Why are more people not freaking out about this? They look at Olaf as a novelty rather than proof that Elsa has the power of a deity. But no. They just keep focusing on the whole "ice thing."

Also, when Elsa moved to the Ice Palace, what did she eat to survive?

81. Ghostbusters 2

I couldn't find plotholes in the first Ghostbusters film, mainly because that film is perfect.

However, Ghostbusters 2 has a plothole that is very common in sequels. Although the Ghostbusters are seen as incompetent charlatans for the majority of the previous movie, they are called upon by the mayor when spectres and demons invade the city. They defeat Gozer the Gozerian moments before the deity brings about the end of the world.

But in Ghostbusters 2, the team has disbanded after society accuses them of being phonies.

How can one single person question the Ghostbuster's legitimacy after people saw thousands of ghosts rampaging around the city? The sky turned black and an earthquake ripped open the ground. How did the Ghostbusters fake that?

They witnessed a skyscraper sized-Stay Puft Marshmallow Man stroll around New York. After the marshmallow man exploded, dozens of people were covered in marshmallow cream. I don't think anyone would forget if that happened to you.

Although the mayor was the one who told the Ghostbusters to save the city from paranormal threats, he dismisses them in this film.

This plothole is also very popular in the Harry Potter series. Harry is an easy target for bullies and is underestimated by his teachers and classmates. Most films in the franchise conclude with Harry saving the day, earning the admiration of everyone around him. Yet, in the following film, it's like everyone's memory has reset as all the students and teachers go right back to bullying Harry as if he isn't a hero.

82. Glass

Kevin Wendell Crumb is institutionalised since he suffers from Dissociative Identity Disorder. Because some of his personalities are hostile, his room has flashing lights that will turn on if Kevin acts inappropriately, forcing him to switch to a more docile personality.

If Kevin doesn't want to experience the effects of the lights, why doesn't he just close his eyes or not look in their direction?

83. Godzilla

As of 2019, there are 35 Godzilla films. In almost every one of these movies, an army attacks Godzilla with guns, tanks, and missiles even though they have proven utterly ineffective against him (excluding the 1998 remake.) If guns, tanks, and missiles are useless against Godzilla, why would the army use the exact same method over 30 times?

84. GoldenEye

In the opening scene, James Bond performs a 722ft bungee jump from a dam to enter the facility. When he exits the building, Bond is on top of a mountain and the dam is nowhere to be seen.

85. Goldfinger
Why does Goldfinger tell the investors his master plan to steal the gold in Fort Knox if he was just going to kill them ten minutes later?

86. The Good Dinosaur
The story revolves around a small Apatosaurus called Arlo. When one of the Apatosauruses achieve their tasks, they put their foot in mud and then smear it on a silo, which is a symbolic way of "leaving their mark."

Due to Arlo's diminutive side, he finds it difficult to perform chores with the same ease as his siblings. His ambition throughout the film is to perform a great feat so he can finally leave his mark on the silo.

There's one problem with this goal. The mud would wash away immediately after it rained.

87. Gravity
The film revolves around astronauts who are trying to survive after their space station crashes into a satellite.

Since there are hundreds of satellites and millions of pieces of space debris in space, you may wonder why this doesn't happen more often.

The reason is simple. Although the film depicts satellites at the same altitude, they are at different altitudes in real life to ensure they can never collide.

There is another error that is very common in space-themed films. Although the stars appear to twinkle from space, stars only do this from Earth's atmosphere.

88. Green Lantern

Hal Jordan joins an intergalactic police force called the Green Lantern Corps, where each member is armed with a Power Ring that can create any construct the wielder imagines. Since the ringbearer is only limited by his or her imagination, the Power Ring is seen as the deadliest weapon in the universe.

After Hal quits the Corps, the Green Lanterns let him keep his ring. This is like if a cop quits the police force but is allowed to keep his gun. Except, instead of a gun, Hal is allowed to keep a Power Ring that can create a tank, a missile, or an atomic bomb.

89. Gremlins

If a Mogwai eats after midnight, it turns into a gremlin. But... it's always after midnight. 8am is after midnight. 11pm is 23 hours after midnight. Is there a certain time where it's okay to feed him? 6am? 9am? If there is, why does nobody mention it to the Mogwai's owners?

90. Guardians of the Galaxy

If the Orb contains the Power Stone, which is one of the most powerful artefacts in the universe, how come nobody is guarding it?

If no one is protecting the Power Stone, why doesn't Thanos take it if he covets it so desperately?

91. Guardians of the Galaxy Vol. 2

The Sovereign's leader, Ayesha hires the Guardians of the Galaxy to exterminate a giant monster. Ayesha tells the Guardians that she does not use her own soldiers to take down the creature because they "cannot risk the lives of our own Sovereign citizens."

After Rocket Raccoon steals batteries from The Sovereign, Ayesha sends a fleet of drones to kill the Guardians. Why didn't Ayesha send these drones to kill the monster?

92. Halloween

How come Michael knows how to drive a car if he has been institutionalised since he was six?

93. Halloween: Resurrection

In the previous film, Halloween: Twenty Years Later, Michael Myers was decapitated by his sister, Laurie Strode... or so it seemed.

In this film, it is unveiled that just before Michael was confronted by Laurie, he put his mask on a paramedic and crushed his larynx so he couldn't tell anyone that he was not Michael Myers. If the paramedic wanted to prove to Laurie that he wasn't Michael, why didn't he just take his mask off?

94. Hancock

This film revolves around an incompetent drunk superhero called John Hancock. Despite the fact that it's common knowledge that Hancock has the same power level as Superman, thugs antagonise him and try to shoot at him.

Why would you threaten or try to injure someone who can effortlessly lift a truck or stop a train? This is a common plothole that revolve around normal people trying to fight superbeings. Criminals always try and shoot Superman and the Hulk even though it's common knowledge that both heroes are bulletproof.

95. The Hangover

Phil, Stu, and Alan wake up from a bachelor's party in Las Vegas, having no memory of the previous night. Having no idea where the bachelor, Doug is, the trio desperately try to retrace their steps to find him. In the end, the three friends find Doug on the roof of their hotel.

Why didn't Doug call for help? Why didn't he bang on the fire escape door? How come a security camera didn't spot him? How is he not at death's door after spending days without food or water while being exposed to the sun's intense heat?

96. Harry Potter and the Philosopher's Stone

In the Harry Potter universe, wizards attend a secret magical school called Hogwarts when they turn 11 years old.

How does that work? If I turned 11 and was invited to Hogwarts, what do I tell my family, friends, schoolmates, neighbours, etc? Kids are going to find it pretty weird when they notice a bunch of students go missing in every school when they are about to enter sixth grade.

You might be thinking that Hogwarts take many precautions to ensure nobody finds out that magic exists.

So how do kids enter Hogwarts? By entering a secret doorway... on Platform 9 at King's Cross railway station.

Do you know how many people pass through that station every year? 33 million! You're telling me not one person at King's Cross saw a kid pass through a secret doorway?

If you want to keep magic a secret, make the kids travel through a station with waaaaaay less people. Narborough station only has 345,360 people per year, which is lower than any other station in Britain. That's a hundred times less people!

Also, why does Voldermort have a nose in this film but he doesn't have one in Harry Potter and the Goblet of Fire?

On top of that, magic isn't real.

97. Harry Potter and the Chamber of Secrets
Why are the Dursleys desperately trying to stop Harry from attending Hogwarts? They hate him. Passionately. Allowing Harry to go to Hogwarts is a perfect opportunity to get rid of him.

98. Harry Potter and the Prisoner of Azkaban
Time-travel is used once in the Harry Potter series to save the hippogriff, Buckbeak.

It is not used to save Harry's parents or the hundreds of people who die in the battle with Voldermort.

99. Harry Potter and the Goblet of Fire

After the students of Hogwarts place their names into the Goblet of Fire, it chooses three of them to compete in the TriWizard Tournament.

However, the Goblet spews out a fourth name – Harry Potter. Harry is too young to compete in the tournament and he never put his name in the Goblet, proving that Voldermort's forces are trying to manipulate the tournament so they can get close enough to him to use his blood to resurrect their master. Despite this, Harry still decides to enter the tournament even though... he doesn't have to. Every wizard knows that dark magic was used to allow Harry to enter the tournament so shouldn't that disqualify him?

Also, this whole plan sounds absurdly convoluted just to get a bit of Harry's blood. Why doesn't his teacher, Mad-Eyed Moody (who is really Voldermort's minion, Barty) ask Harry for his blood for a spell and then use it to resurrect Voldermort?

100. Harry Potter and the Order of the Phoenix

A thestral is a creature that can only be seen by someone who has witnessed death. Although thestrals have been around Hogwarts since Harry joined the school, he can only see them now because he watched Cedric die in the events that occurred during the previous movie.

However, Harry saw Voldermort kill his mother when he was a baby. Harry Potter author, JK Rowling explained that he wouldn't have been able to see the thestrals before Cedric's death because Harry was too young to remember his mother's demise.

This theory completely falls apart since Harry saw Quirrel die in the first movie.

101. Harry Potter and the Half-Blood Prince
Why does Harry Potter read a magical newspaper in front of non-magical people in the first scene?

Just to be as unsubtle as possible, he holds it up so everyone who walks by can see the pictures moving on the newspaper, so they can see it's magical. Considering Harry is meant to be the chosen one, he's a bit stupid.

102. Harry Potter and the Deathly Hallows Part 1
According to the story of The Deathly Hallows, a man cheated Death with an invisibility cloak. Since Death couldn't see the man while he wore the cloak, Death couldn't claim his life.

Eventually, the man gave the cloak to his son. Without the cloak, Death was allowed to claim the man's soul.

This story implies that the man could never take off the cloak or Death would appear to claim his life.

That means this man had a child with a woman... while he was invisible. How long was he wearing it for? Ten years? Longer? And it never slipped off once? Not even when he was going to the toilet or something? I have so many questions.

103. Harry Potter and the Deathly Hallows Part 2

This is a really small mistake but it is so easy to avoid, it's worth mentioning. In a flashback, we see Harry's mother, Lilly.

Despite the fact that Snape said that Harry has his mother's blue eyes, Lilly clearly has brown eyes. How difficult was it to find a girl with blue eyes to play that character?

104. Hellboy

When FBI Agent, John Myer enters the Bureau of Paranormal Research and Defence, he finds himself in a library that seems to be empty.

He then hears a voice that tells him to "turn the pages." Myer sees that there is an aquatic creature called Abe Sapien inside a fish tank. Myer realises that Abe is reading a book located outside the tank but the creature can't turn the pages without getting out of the water.

Although it's a cool reveal, it doesn't make any sense. Was Abe just waiting all day for someone to turn the page for him? It must take him forever to read anything!

Also, we learn later that Abe can live outside of water. So why didn't he get out of the tank himself to turn the pages?

105. Hercules

The Green god of the underworld, Hades wishes to rule Zeus' domain, Olympus. To ensure his plan succeeds, Hades sends his minions, Pain and Panic to kill Zeus' son, Hercules. Although Pain and Panic fail to kill Hercules, Hades believes they succeeded. Hades doesn't learn for many years that Hercules is still alive.

But if Hades is the god of the underworld, that means he guards all souls. So why doesn't check to see if he has Hercules' soul? Although he has a bajillion souls, it wouldn't be difficult for him to find a specific one since he easily finds Megaera's soul later in the film.

Also, Hades allies with The Faiths; three witches who decide who dies and when. Surely, they could have told Hades that Hercules was still alive.

106.   The Hitman's Bodyguard
When the war criminal, Dukhovich learns that the hitman, Kincaid is expected to testify against him, Dukhovich does everything in his power to have him killed. Despite Dukhovich's efforts, Kincaid reaches the courtroom and provides a password for a secure website that shows pictures of the war criminal committing acts of terrorism.

However, if Kincaid knew the password, he could have provided it to the court through a phone call. I mean... the movie would be over in five minutes but still...

107.   The Hobbit: The Unexpected Journey
Bilbo Baggins's blade, Sting glows when orcs and goblins are nearby.

However, there are numerous scenes throughout The Hobbit trilogy where you can clearly see Sting is not glowing when goblins are nearby.

108.   The Hobbit: The Desolation of Smaug
At the end of the previous film, The Eagles rescued Bilbo and his allies from the orcs and flew them to safety. As The Eagles leave Bilbo

and his company, they continue their journey to Smaug's domain, Erebor.

Why didn't the Eagles just fly Bilbo straight to Erebor?

109. The Hobbit: The Battle of the Five Armies

After Smaug is defeated, a battle between humans, elves, orcs, dwarves, and Eagles initiates. The dwarf leader, Thorin is terrified someone will plunder the gold from his domain and so, prevents his group from engaging in the fight.

When the orcs appear to be winning the fight, Thorin finally comes to his senses. He and his band of 12 dwarves leave their domain and charge into the battlefield and help defeat the orcs.

Although this is supposed to be a powerful moment, how are 13 dwarves going to make a difference in a battle of this magnitude? During this fight, thousands of elves (that have been trained in combat for centuries) are slaughtered by orcs. How does 13 dwarves turn the tide of battle?

110. Home Alone

Kevin McCallister is left at home alone while two robbers desperately try to break in. At no point in the entire film does Kevin attempt to call his parents or the police.

You might think to yourself, 'Yeah, but that's because the power was knocked out on the night before his flight.' If the phone isn't working, how did he order a pizza?

Also, he rings the police at the end of the film (but only after the burglars break in.)

111.   Home Alone 2: Lost in New York
Kevin gets on the wrong flight and accidentally flies to New York. The criminals from the last film, Harry and Marv happen to arrive in New York on the same day as Kevin and they bump into each other shortly after.

First off, what are the odds that the criminals and Kevin would be in the exact same place at the exact same time? Even if they were in New York, what are the chances they would bump into each other in a city with a population of eight million?

112.   Hook
Peter Pan tells Tinkerbell that he ran away from his family when he was a baby because he didn't want to live in a world filled with death. This inspired him to go to Neverland.

How does a baby have any understanding over the concept of death?

Also, if Tinkerbell brought Peter Pan to a world where he will never grow up, why does he keep getting older?

113. Ice Age
Sid the sloth appears in all five Ice Age movies. What are sloths best-known for? Being slow. They are the laziest mammals in the world apart from koalas.

However, Sid doesn't display this behaviour throughout the franchise. In fact, he's much faster than most of the main characters. Why make a character a sloth if he's not going to be slow?

114. Ice Age: Dawn of Dinosaurs
The first two films in the Ice Age franchise take place around 10,000 years ago.

This film takes place at the dawn of the dinosaurs... who first appeared 235 million years ago and went extinct 65 million years ago.

I know it's silly to nit-pick a children's movie but children have a rough idea of the timeframe when the Ice Age happened and when the dinosaurs went extinct.

115. Inception
Dom Cobb is an extractor who can enter a person's mind and steal their ideas. After Cobb

was falsely accused of murdering his wife, he fled the country to avoid being arrested.

Desperate to return home to see his children, Cobb agrees to perform a mindheist for a powerful businessman called Saito. If Cobb is successful, Saito guarantees that the charges against Cobb will be quashed, allowing him to return home to his family. To perform this heist, Cobb and his group must enter a dream within a dream within a dream within a dream of a person.

Instead of going through this absurdly complicated plan, why doesn't Cobb have his kids flown out to him? That's way easier that going inside a dream inside a dream inside a dream inside a dream of a person.

116. The Incredibles

In most superhero stories, the villain believes he will emerge triumphant due to their doomsday weapon, not realising that it has a glaring weakness that the superhero exploits.

To get around this, the supervillain, Syndrome forces superheroes to defeat his killer robot, The Omnidroid, so he can rebuilt it so it is immune to the previous way it was defeated.

After rebuilding The Omnidroid nine times, it is now immune to lava, magnetism, electricity, etc. In the final battle, the Incredibles manage to defeat The Omnidroid by tricking it into penetrating its own armour with its tentacles, pulling out its CPU.

However, this is exactly how it was defeated the previous time. Why didn't Syndrome make The Omnidroid's shell denser than its tentacles? If he did, the robot would have been unbeatable.

117. The Incredibles 2

After The Incredibles fail to stop the supervillain, The Underminer, they receive a lot of bad PR and are forced to stay at a crummy motel.

Soon after, a wealthy businessman called Winston Deavor sets up a meeting with Mr. Incredible and Elastigirl. Winston believes superheroes can be legal again if the public see The Incredibles in a positive light.

However, Winston's sister, Evelyn intends to tarnish the superheroes' reputation beyond repair.

So why does she help her brother hire The Incredibles in the first place? The Incredibles' reputation was already in tatters after their battle with The Underminer, causing millions of dollars worth of damage.

Also, Evelyn's plan is to ensure being a superhero is illegal... even though they are already illegal.

118. Independence Day
After a group of UFOs wipe out many of the world's biggest cities, the humans attack them, only to learn that the spacecrafts are protected by impenetrable shields. A satellite technician called David Levinson solves this problem by sending a virus to the aliens' mothership using his Mac.

How can an Apple Mac be compatible with an alien spacecraft? Do they use the same software?

119. Indiana Jones and the Temple of Doom
Realizing that their plane is about to crash, Indy, Willie, and Short Round jump out of the vehicle on an inflatable raft and plummet hundreds of feet below. They then slide off a cliff and drop hundreds of feet (again) into a river.

Not only do they survive two separate drops of hundreds of feet, none of them fall out of the raft at any point. It would have been more realistic if they stayed on the plane and survived the crash.

120. Indiana Jones and the Kingdom of the Crystal Skull
Everyone mocks the scene where Indy survives a nuclear blast by hiding inside a refrigerator. The director argued that Indy would have been protected from the radiation by the fridge's lead-casing.

Firstly, the blast launches the fridge into the air by at least a hundred feet. Hitting the ground from that high should turn Indy into paste.

Also, when he gets out of the fridge, he is still in the radius of the blast so the radiation should poison him.

Although many viewers have acknowledged these plotholes, there is another one that many people miss. Before 1956 (one year before the story takes place,) fridge doors had latches making them impossible to open from the inside. Even if Indy could have survived the blast, he should have been trapped inside the fridge... forever.

121. Inglourious Basterds

Hugo Stiglitz was known throughout Germany for killing 13 Gestapo officers and defecting to the US. However, not one German notices him while he and the rest of the Basterds enter a Nazi bar.

122. Inside Out

Joy and Sadness must return to Riley's Headquarters and reinsert her Core Emotion before she suffers irreversible damage.

On their journey, they bump into two workers who are in charge of Riley's memories. They tell Joy that they send one random memory of a

Tripledent Gum Commercial up to Headquarters just for fun.

The workers are admitting they have direct access to Headquarters, which means Joy and Sadness can return there the same way.

Since the workers send the memory through a thin tube, it's possible that Joy and Sadness may not fit.

If that was the case, Joy could still send the Core Emotions through the tube so Anger, Fear, and Disgust can insert them into their designated slots. If this 30-second gag wasn't in the film, the plothole would have been avoided.

123. Interstellar

The characters repeatedly emphasise that Matt Damon's character, Dr. Hugh Mann, is the smartest astronaut at NASA.

Despite his unquestionable genius, Mann didn't know that opening an air lock would depressurize the room, blowing it up.

And you can't argue that Mann forgot because Cooper TELLS him not to open the air lock. I'm not an astronaut and I know that!

124. Iron Man

Obadiah Stane steals Tony Stark's arc reactor in his chest after using a high-pitched frequency that causes paralysis to anyone who hears it.

I don't understand why every supervillain is desperate for Iron Man's tech when Stane's paralysing frequency tech is WAY better! You could use that against a group of terrorists. You could defeat an entire army without a single life being lost. You could have used that tech to defeat Thanos in Avengers: Infinity War in 30 seconds.

125. Iron Man 2
Whiplash walks onto the track of the Grand Prix de Monaco to kill Tony Stark who is driving one of the cars.

But Tony only decided at the last minute to take part in the race. If Tony didn't decide to race, how did Whiplash intend to kill him?

126. Iron Man 3
A terrorist called The Mandarin admits to a bombing that critically injures Tony Stark's friend, Happy Hogan.

To prove he is not scared of The Mandarin, Tony Stark tells the terrorist to come for him next. Tony then brazenly broadcasts his home address on live-television so The Mandarin knows exactly where to find him.

Now, I can understand why Tony would does this since he's arrogant and believes he's untouchable.

But what's ludicrous is that he takes absolutely no precautions to guard his house. No weapons. No shields. No Avengers. Nothing. Although Tony launches over 40 Iron Man suits simultaneously in the film's conclusion, he doesn't activate them to guard his mansion while he and his lover are inside, even though he knows an attack is imminent. Despite the fact that Tony is one of the smartest people in the world, he can be a real idiot.

127. IT

Pennywise the Clown is an interdimensional shapeshifter that feeds off fear. Because children experience the most intense form of fear, he usually eats kids. To lure children, Pennywise takes the form of something that kids like – a clown.

But in this film, Pennywise looks like the most terrifying clown possible. The clowns in the film, Killer Klowns from Space looked less scary. No kid will go 100ft towards a clown that looks like Pennywise. If he wanted to lure kids in, why didn't he take the form of a puppy or a kitten or a clown that looks human.

128. Jaws

After it is confirmed that a shark has killed two people in Amity Island, the police chief, Brody orders for the beach to be shut down. Worried that this will devastate the town's economy, the mayor refuses.

However, closing the beach shouldn't be the problem. If the beach wasn't closed, why would anyone go there when there was, not one, but two shark attacks? Even if a tourist desperately wanted to go there, why wouldn't they just go to another beach that... y'know... doesn't have man-killing sharks?

Also, sharks only eat five people per year. The reason why sharks don't eat people is because they don't like the taste of human flesh. You are more likely to be killed by a vending machine or a donkey than a shark.

129. Jaws IV: The Revenge

In the final scene, the shark roars... despite the fact that sharks don't have lungs.

130. Jumanji

After Sarah Whittle witnesses Robin William's character, Alan Parrish, being sucked into the board game of Jumanji, she tells the police and her parents. Nobody believes her and so, everyone in the town accuses Sarah of being crazy, which forces her to change her name.

What's the point of changing your name... if you live in the same town in the same house?

Everybody still knows who you are! How is that going to fool anybody?

131. Jurassic Park

Nedry is a computer expert at Jurassic Park who deactivates the security system to steal dinosaur DNA so he can sell it to the park's rival company. When the park's analysts try to reactivate the system, a picture of Nedry appears on the computer, taunting them since they don't know the password.

By doing this, Nedry is admitting to his crimes. Why would Nedry leave a paper trail? Does Nedry realise that he has to now go into hiding forever?

132. Jurassic Park: The Lost World

When the T-Rex is transported to the US, it kills everyone onboard the ship. When the vessel docks, the T-Rex breaks out of its cargo hold.

Wait, so the T-Rex broke out, killed everyone, went back into its' cargo hold, then locked himself in?

133. Jurassic World

Everyone knows the premise of the Jurassic Park franchise. Hammond clones dinosaurs to create a prehistoric amusement park. Although Hammond emphasises that he has spared no expense, the dinosaurs escape and go on a killing spree. In the sequels, more dinosaurs are cloned

Despite how disastrous Hammond's park was, scientists keep cloning dinosaurs and keep trying to make Jurassic Parks.

Here's the thing – Over 90% of dinosaurs were vegetarian including sauropods like the brachiosaurus, Apatosaurus, and brontosaurus. Why don't the scientists just clone the vegetarian dinosaurs? Sauropods don't eat people and are larger than a football stadium which is WAY more impressive than a velociraptor (which was about 1ft tall in real life.)

So, if you had to clone dinosaurs, clone the ones that don't eat people and you might actually make a profit for once.

134. Jurassic World: Fallen Kingdom

The main characters meet Benjamin Lockwood, who was John Hammond's partner when he was constructing Jurassic Park. A little girl called Maisie is introduced as Lockwood's granddaughter.

It is later revealed that Maisie is a clone of Lockwood's daughter and she was created with the same technology that Hammond used to clone the dinosaurs.

The big question is – Why do people care about cloning dinosaurs if you can literally cheat death through cloning humans? This is a question nobody asks in this film.

Instead of pursuing the greatest scientific breakthrough in history, Hammond and his team decided to set up a Jurassic Park FIVE TIMES, even though every one of them ended in bloodshed.

135. Justice League

Aquaman calls Bruce Wayne "Bátman" in front of a group of civilians. While dressed as Batman, Bruce Wayne refers to his butler by his real name. When Lois Lane sees Superman, she calls him "Clark." Does ANYONE in this film understand the concept of a secret identity?

136. The Karate Kid

In the tournament, the referee emphasises that a contestant will be eliminated if they kick their opponent in the face.

How does Daniel win the tournament? By kicking his opponent in the face. Why did the writers make this rule if Daniel was going to break it in the final scene?

137. Kick-Ass

Dave Lizewski loves comic books so much, he decides to become a superhero called Kick-Ass.

Believing he needs a costume, Dave orders an outfit and mask from a scuba website.

Although no one can figure out Kick-Ass' identity, it should be pretty easy since the company would have a record of the addresses its products have been sent to. It would be like if Batman bought his Batsuit through Amazon and was surprised if someone figured out his identity.

138. Kill Bill
The Bride has the ability to kill anyone with the Five-Point Palm Exploding Heart Technique. She chooses never to use this at any point except in the final battle in Kill Bill Vol. 2.

139. Kung Fu Panda
There are two flashback scenes showing Oogway rejecting Tai Lung. However, the two scenes don't match. How did the animators make that mistake? In fact, it requires MORE work to screw this up! Instead of animating a scene and then copying and pasting it, the animators had to create two different scenes that are meant to be the same scene.

140. The LEGO Movie
It is revealed in the conclusion that the events in this film take place in a child's imagination.

However, we then see the Lego character, Emmett move in the real world.

So... it doesn't take place in a child's imagination and Lego figures are alive? Which is it? Make up your mind, movie!

141. The Lion King

After Scar takes over Pride Rock, all the rivers and lakes dry up and the grass stops growing...... but how? Is it because Scar allowed the hyenas into Pride Rock? Hyenas are carnivores, which means they don't eat plants. So, who ate all the grass? Did the hyenas drink the water from every river?

At the beginning of the film, we see elephants in Pride Rock. Elephants drink 160 litres of water daily. Are you telling me a bunch of hyenas can drink more water than an elephant?

Even if they accomplished this (somehow,) wouldn't the water return after it rained? Does Scar have magical weather powers?

Also, how does all the grass and water return to Pride Rock when Scar is defeated?

142. The Little Mermaid

Although Ariel is in love with Prince Eric, she can't be with him because she is a mermaid. She makes a deal with the witch, Ursula to be transformed into a human in exchange for her voice. Since she can't speak, Ariel can't explain her situation to Prince Eric.

So why doesn't she just write something down? That would've have cleared up the situation way faster.

Also, she doesn't seem bothered that Prince Eric eats seafood considering Ariel's friend, Flounder is a fish.

143. Logan

When Nurse Lopez learns her co-workers are performing horrific experiments on children, she hires Logan to escort one of the kids, Laura to a safehouse.

Lopez records the atrocities that occur in this facility on her phone.

Despite shooting the footage on a regular phone, her video has seamless editing and narration. This means Lopez taped several videos on her phone, uploaded them to her computer, used editing software like iMovie to stitch the clips together, record narration over the stitched clip, and then transfer that file back to her phone.

Also, how is she able to get into the most secure rooms? Where are the security guards?

If she survived, Lopez probably would have become the world's greatest documentarian.

144. Looper

If the mob want to dispose of a person, they will use a time machine to send them into the past where they are killed by an assassin called a looper. The last person that the looper kills is a future version of themselves to "close the loop" to avoid any ties to the mob.

However, loopers sometimes panic when confronted with the future version of themselves which causes them to escape. This happens to the lead character, Joe and his worker, Seth.

To avoid this from happening, why doesn't the mob send the person back in time to the bottom of the ocean or in a coffin? Why don't the mob kill the person and THEN send them back in time?

145. The Lord of the Rings: The Fellowship of the Ring

When Gandalf grows suspicious of Bilbo's magical ring, he leaves The Shire to research it. After several months, he concludes it is The One Ring, which belongs to the dark lord, Sauron.

However, Gandalf should have known it was The One Ring immediately since he saw The Eye of Sauron when he tried to pick it up.

This is a plothole that is exasperated by the prequel, The Hobbit, as we see Gandalf confront

Sauron so there is no way he would mistake The Eye of Sauron as anything else.

146. The Lord of the Rings: The Two Towers
Legolas tells Aragorn that a red sun rises which means that "blood has been spilt this night."

What does that mean? Are you tell me that the sun only turns red when someone dies that same night? Thousands of people die every day. How does that work?

147. The Lord of the Rings: Return of the King

The One Ring can only be destroyed in the fires of Mount Doom. Instead of travelling to the volcano on foot for over a year, many viewers stated that Gandalf could have flown on one of the Eagles to Mount Doom. The Eagles would have reached their destination in a few days.

However, this "plothole" has a perfect explanation. Gandalf entrusted a hobbit with The One Ring because they are considered to be the purest beings and so, are the least likely to be corrupted by the Ring's evil.

If The Eagles or Gandalf were corrupted by The One Ring, the birds would have flown straight to Sauron's castle and he would've reclaimed his power.

So, there you go. The trilogy's biggest plothole isn't a plothole after all.

However, there is one plothole that nobody can argue with. If Mount Doom is the only place in Middle Earth that can destroy The One Ring, why isn't it guarded? Why doesn't Sauron have Nazgul, orcs, mumakil, were-worms, Uruk-Hai, wargs, Shelob, and a Balrog or two protecting the volcano?

Why doesn't Saruman hire a few trolls to seal up the doorway to Mount Doom? He could have at least built a gate or something!

148. Man of Steel

Since Zod is a Kryptonian like Superman, he has superstrength and can fly when exposed to a yellow Sun. Zod attempts to use The World Engine to terraform the Earth so his species will revert to normal. Unfortunately, the terraforming will kill everyone on Earth.

Why does Zod want to rid himself of his superpowers? He can fly in space, lift a building, shoot lasers from his eyes, and freeze things with his breath. Why give that up? It would make more sense if he used his god-like power to rule over humanity.

Also, if Zod has the power to alter a planet's atmosphere, why doesn't he terraform a world that isn't guarded by Superman? What's wrong with Mars? If he terraformed Mars, I'm pretty sure the inhabitants of Earth would have been cool with that.

Also, in the final fight, Zod says, "There's only one way this can end, Kal-El. Either you die or I do."

Em... Zod... there are clearly two ways that can go. You were a great general but I'll assume maths wasn't your strongest subject.

149. The Matrix

Although Morpheus and his crews are trying to defeat the Agents, we learn that his crewmember, Cypher has betrayed the team and is seen meeting Agent Smith in The Matrix.

This should be impossible since a person can't plug in and out of The Matrix without an operator.

Although this is considered to be the biggest plothole in The Matrix (at least in the first movie,) it has a simple explanation. According to the directors, Cypher isn't in The Matrix in this scene. He is in a separate program and has allowed Agent Smith access to it. Cypher has tweaked the program so he can go in and out of it without an operator. This is why he acts paranoid when Neo enters the room just before Cypher jacks into the program.

Now, this doesn't mean that The Matrix is not devoid of plotholes. After Neo has the bug ripped out of his bellybutton, how is he... you know... alive? At the very least, how is he not in excruciating pain?

Just before that scene, Morpehus rings Neo to tell him to meet under the Adams Saint bridge but he has to be quick since Agents have tapped the phone. If the Agents knew Neo was going to the Adams Saint bridge, why didn't they show up there?

Also, you can't resurrect someone with a kiss of love. That's just silly.

150. The Matrix Reloaded

Trinity is mortally wounded by an Agent while falling from a skyscraper. Since Neo is miles away, he has to fly at supersonic speed to catch her before she hits the ground. We see Neo move so quickly, the shockwave shatters glass and lifts up dozens of vehicles into the air.

When Neo catches her, shouldn't the impact obliterate her since he is moving faster than a fighter jet?

Some people would argue, "In The Matrix, some rules can be bent or broken." But minutes before this scene, we see a single punch from an Agent causes Trinity to bleed internally. If a punch can cause that much damage, I can't imagine what would happen if Neo grabbed her while moving that quickly.

151. The Matrix Revolutions

After Neo passed out at the end of the previous movie, he is brought to the infirmary. While he is unconscious, his mind goes to a place called The Train Station. After he is rescued by Trinity, Neo says he needs to see the Oracle before he leaves.

Wait, how can Neo visit the Oracle? He's not in The Matrix, remember? He's in a different program.

After he leaves the Oracle, we see Neo being unplugged from The Matrix... but he wasn't jacked into the Matrix in the first place! He was in the infirmary beforehand, remember?

This mistake could have been fixed if Neo said he needs to see the Oracle AFTER he leaves The Train Station. However, we hear Neo state that he must meet the Oracle BEFORE he leaves there so this is unmistakably a plothole.

152. Maximum Overdrive

Okay, this film is about killer automobiles so it can't be taken seriously. However, there's an error that is so ridiculous, I had to include it. In the beginning of the film, it is stated the machines came to life after being exposed to radiation from a passing comet.

This is contradicted in the epilogue when it is stated that the machines were brought to life because of a UFO laser.

If the film didn't have an epilogue, it would have made more sense... okay, it wouldn't because cars can't come to life but it would have made slightly more sense.

153. The Meg

Jason Statham's character, Jonas says he recognises the Megalodon shark that terrorises the oceans throughout the film because he saw it years before.

This is impossible because we see the Meg being released from under a gas seal by a submarine. How could Jonas have seen the Meg if it was trapped under the seal for millions of years?

154. Memento

Leonard is trying to find out who killed his wife despite the fact he has amnesia that causes his memory to fade every 15 minutes. Trying to piece the mystery together, he takes pictures, writes pivotal information on his notes, and tattoos suspects' names on his body. Throughout the movie, many people take advantage of Leonard's disability for their own gain.

However, Leonard could have avoided being manipulated by simply recording conversations.

Also, if he can't remember anything... how does Leonard remember he has amnesia?

155. Men in Black

When Agent J is inducted into The Men in Black, he sees a floating orb in one of the offices and pokes it out of curiosity, causing it to fly around the facility. When Agent K catches it, he says the orb is so dangerous, it "caused the 1977 New York black out."

If it's so dangerous, why is out in the open? Shouldn't be in a safe or something? You could have least put up a sign that said, "Don't touch."

156. Men in Black III

Agent K deployed an ArcNet in 1969, preventing aliens from penetrating Earth. When the Boglodite, Boris the Animal goes back in time and kills K before he deploys the ArcNet, it allows his species to invade Earth.

Agent J goes back in time and prevents Agent K's assassination, allowing him to deploy the ArcNet.

But if there is an ArcNet blocking aliens from entering Earth's atmosphere, how did extra-terrestrials invade the planet in the events in the last two films?

157. Minority Report

John Anderton uses technology called PreCrime to learn when murders will take place hours before they occur.

After an insider manipulates the system, Anderton is accused of killing someone within the next 24 hours. Although PreCrime police usually don't know the exact circumstances of the future murder, Anderton knows the location and time of the crime that he is supposed to commit.

So why doesn't he just drive in the opposite direction of his future victim, proving that the system has been manipulated?

158. Mission: Impossible

Probably the most iconic moment in the Mission: Impossible franchise is when Tom Cruise's character, Ethan Hunt is lowered on a wire into a security room. The room is so secure, it will activate the alarm if it feels a change in temperature, sound, or if someone touches the ground.

However, there was a much easier way to stop people from entering the room. One word – cameras. Even the most rudimentary banks have security cameras.

159. Mission: Impossible II
During the motorcycle chase, Ethan Hunt and Ambrose drive their bikes at each other at top speed. When they crash into one another, Hunt and Ambrose jump off the bikes and collide into each other, falling onto a beach where they fight to the death.

I know the word "impossible" is in the title but you can't expect me to believe that a human travelling at 100mph can collide into a person travelling towards them at 100mph without them both dying instantly. Neither of them even broke a bone!

160. Mission: Impossible III
Throughout the Mission: Impossible franchise, the spy group, IMF make realistic masks to impersonate important figures to help them break into secure locations.

In Mission: Impossible III, Ethan Hunt creates a mask of Philip Seymour Hoffman's character, Davian.

However, the two men's appearance and build are so different, it would be impossible for Hunt to impersonate Davian. It doesn't matter how realistic the mask is since it's not going to change the shape of the person's teeth, jaw, height, build, posture, or weight.

161. Mission: Impossible - Ghost Protocol
The most iconic moment in the film is when Ethan climbs on the outside of the world's tallest building, the 2,722ft Burj Khalifa.

Despite the fact Ethan climbs 11 stories on the exterior of the Burj Khalifa, not one person inside the building seems him.

162. Mission: Impossible – Rogue Nation
Ethan Hunt needs to access a hard-drive in an underwater room. However, the cooling system has an alarm that will activate if there is metal near the hard-drive, meaning that it's impossible for a person to dive into this room with an oxygen tank. Since it takes three minutes to get in and out of the room, it should be impossible to access the hard-drive. Ethan Hunt accomplishes this because he is awesome.

However, the idea that the cooling system can detect metal is contradicted since Hunt clearly uses a computer on his sleeve.

163. Mission: Impossible - Fallout
When Ethan Hunt is being chased by criminals, he jumps into a sewer where his companions, Luther and Benji are waiting for him on a boat.

How did Luther and Benji know to wait for Ethan there? Just before he jumped into the sewer, Ethan got knocked off his motorcycle by a car. Because of this, it looks like Ethan got knocked off his bike ON PURPOSE so he could meet Benji and Luther at that spot.

164. Monsters, Inc.

The Monsters do everything in their power to ensure humanity does not learn of their existence.

So how does the chairman punish Mike and Sully for breaking the law? Abandoning them on Earth, where they will be discovered by humanity, proving that monsters exist.

165. Ocean's Eleven

Danny Ocean intends to steal $150 million from a casino's bank vault. During the heist, he leaves half the money in the vault but arms it with explosives. He tells the casino's owner, Benedict that he will detonate the bombs unless Ocean can walk out with the other half.

Although Benedict agrees, it is revealed that the "money" that Ocean left in the vault is hooker flyers and he had stolen ALL of the cash.

However, there was no point where Ocean could have put the cases of flyers in the vault.

166. Pacific Rim

The film revolves around a portal under the ocean that spews out Godzilla-sized monsters called Kaiju. Since the monsters cannot be harmed with conventional weapons, humanity builds skyscraper-sized robots called Jaegars to battle the Kaiju.

Although the robots have great difficulty defeating the creatures, there is one scene where a Jaegar decapitates a Kaiju with a sword that is built into his arm. Not only has this sword not used before, it is never used again despite being the most effective weapon against the Kaiju.

167. Paranormal Activity
If a house is possessed… leave.

168. Pirates of the Caribbean: Curse of the Black Pearl
The pirates of the Black Pearl are cursed so food turns to ash in their mouths. So why do they have food on their ship?

169. Pirates of the Caribbean: Salazar's Revenge
Jack Sparrow releases the ghost of Salazar from his prison after he gives away his cursed compass.

However, Sparrow gave this compass to Elizabeth and Will Turner in previous films without suffering any consequences.

170. Planet of the Apes (2001)
The film takes place on an alien planet. So... how does an alien planet... have horses? Where did they come from?

I know the ending bothers a lot of people for being non-sensical but the horses bother me way more.

171. Pocahontas
Okay, it's common knowledge that Pocahontas was only a child when John Smith and The Settlers arrived in America. I'm not going to criticise that because the film has to tweak a few details to make the story work.

What I do have a problem with is when Ratcliffe lands, he holds up the United Kingdom flag. Although this film takes place in 1607, this flag (which is called the Union Jack,) didn't exist until 1801.

What makes this inconsistency more frustrating is they show the correct flag at the beginning of the film!

172. Point Break
Keanu Reeves' character, Johnny Utah dreamed of being a professional footballer until he suffered a severe knee injury in college. When he left college, Utah became an FBI agent. Near the end of the film, Utah chases a criminal called

Bodhi. As Utah leaps off a wall, he keels over due to his knee injury. How come Utah can't jump from an 8ft wall but he passed the most rigorous physical training possible to join the FBI? Also, if his injury was so severe, why was Utah assigned to a mission where he has to surf, chase criminals, and skydive?

173. Poltergeist
If a house is possessed… don't invite more people into it.

174. Predator
When Dutch learns that the Predator only attacks people who are armed, he tells Anna not to pick up her weapon. Once Dutch realises this, why doesn't everybody drop their weapons?

175. The Princess and the Frog
Prince Naveen has been turned into a frog and will only revert to human if he is kissed by a princess.

If a non-princess kisses him, she will be turned into a frog.

But when Naveen is kissed by Charlotte at the end of the film, she remains human. There is no explanation why Charlotte doesn't turn into a frog.

176. Prometheus

Prometheus is considered to be one of the most plothole-filled films in recent memory. However, most of these plotholes were covered by the YouTube channel, RedLetterMedia, so I will try to avoid pointing out the same inconsistencies.

Okay, let's look at the story. A spaceship called the Prometheus flies through space to find a race of aliens called Engineers who are actually the creators of life on Earth.

The crew travels with an android called David. Later, it is revealed that David has an ulterior motive and begins sabotaging the mission and infecting the crew for... no reason. David literally has nothing to gain by jeopardising the mission.

In the original script, David was meant to turn evil after his creator, Peter Weyland activated a secret program in the android. However, since this was removed from the film, David's motivation doesn't make any sense.

In the film's climax, the Engineer's ship crashes onto the ground. Many viewers noticed that the wrecked ship looks almost exactly like the wrecked ship in Alien. Also, the first Xenomorph is born on this moon so it reconfirms it is the same moon that the crew visited in the original film. Although Prometheus is criticised for its plotholes, this seems like a very nice piece of continuity.

But there's a problem. The moon that the crew land on in this film is called LV-223. The moon in Alien is called LV-426. So how did the Xenomorphs and Engineer ship get to the other moon? It's never explained. So, the director had a perfect opportunity to connect the two films but decided not to.

177. The Purge
The premise for The Purge is simple – In the United States, all crime is legal once a year from 7pm-7am. During this time, many people barricade themselves in their homes, hoping that no one will break in.

There has never been an explanation why these characters simply don't book a flight to any country in the world on the week of The Purge.

178. Raiders of the Lost Ark
When the Nazis kidnap Marion and escape on a submarine, Indy stows away on the vehicle. However, he doesn't get the chance to open the hatch so Indy has to hold his breathe while hanging onto the top of the sub.

The vessel travels from the middle of the Mediterranean Sea all the way to an island in the Aegean Sea. This journey takes about 50 hours.

Just to remind you, humans can hold their breath for four minutes. Look, some moments in the Indiana Jones are a little unrealistic.

Surviving falling off a cliff.

Surviving falling out of a plane.

Making archaeology interesting.

But I cannot believe that Indy can hold his breath 750 times longer than a normal person.

Just to make this scenario more confusing, Indy has already arrived on the island before the sub docks! How did he get there before the submarine? Is he Aquaman?

179. Ralph Breaks the Internet

In the beginning of the film, Ralph plays Tron with Vanellope even though the game has a virus.

However, they are playing the game in an arcade. How can an arcade game get a virus? Better still, how did the director make a movie about video games without knowing how video games work?

180. Ready Player One

The film takes place in 2045 where people seek escape from the dystopian world by entering a virtual reality called the Oasis. If a person finds three hidden Eastern Eggs in the simulation, they will be able to control the entire Oasis. Although the first Easter Egg is hidden on a racetrack, no one has been able to complete it in five years. The protagonist, Wade Watts learns that the only way to beat the track is to drive backwards from the starting point.

How has no one ever thought of that in five years? Everyone who has played Mario Kart has tried going backwards to find a shortcut or secret area at some point.

Also, why does the CEO of the biggest tech company on Earth, Sorrento leave his password right beside his VR chair? What if someone uses that password to hack his VR helmet (which is exactly what happens.) How has Sorrento not memorised his own password? Why doesn't he hide it somewhere more inconspicuous?

181. Rear Window

While Jeff is bound in a wheelchair, he becomes bored and spends his days studying his neighbours. When he suspects that his neighbour, Thorwald is a killer, he confides his suspicions to Detective Doyle.

When Thorwald learns that Jeff is onto him, he confronts Jeff, preparing to murder him. As Thorwald approaches him, Jeff takes pictures of Thorwald with a flashbulb, blinding him. Jeff does this four times, stunning Thorwald each time.

At no point does Thorwald try to shield his eyes, look away, or run towards Jeff at top speed.

Basically, a paralysed man defeats a murderer by taking pictures of him. This is literally the conclusion of one of the greatest films ever made.

182. Reservoir Dogs

The film concludes with Mr. White, Nice Guy Eddy, and Joe shooting each other during a Mexican stand-off.

If you look at the shoot-out closely, it doesn't make sense. Mr. White points his gun at Joe. Nice Guy Eddy and Joe point their gun at Mr. White. When Mr. White fires his gun, Joe and Nice Guy Eddie drop dead, even though nobody was aiming at Eddie.

183. The Ring

The ghost, Samara kills her victims by coming out of their TV. How do you stop her? Break the tv... or just don't have a tv.

184. Rocky

Rocky knocks out Apollo Creed in the first round after 55 seconds. Creed gets up before the count of 10... according to the film. In reality, Creed didn't get up until the count of 15 if not more. Rocky should have won in the first round.

185. Rocky II
While training, Rocky runs 30 miles non-stop, which would make him one of the greatest sprinters in history.

Nevertheless, no one addresses this. Someone should say, "Dude, why don't you become a marathon runner? Also, how did you run that much with zero training or preparation?"

186. Rocky IV
During a demonstration of his strength, the Soviet boxer, Ivan Drago punches a machine that monitors his power. The machine gauges that Drago punches with a force of 2,150lbs per square inch.

That. Is. Impossible. The average force of a boxer's punch is 800lbs PSI. The strongest punch ever recorded was 1,300lbs PSI, which is not even close to what Drago is capable of.

However, I had to give this film a little slack since the actor who portrays Drago, Dolph Lundgren is so strong in real life, he burst a cardial sac in Sylvester Stallone's heart while they were filming a scene. According to Stallone's doctor, he was hit with the same impact as "head-on a collision with a car." Okay, nobody can punch 2,150lbs PSI but Lundgren is still really, really, really strong.

187. Rocky V

In the previous film, Rocky's son is eight. Despite the fact this film takes place immediately after Rocky IV ends, Rocky's son is now a teenager.

188. Rogue One

In Star Wars, the Death Star is destroyed when Luke Skywalker fires at its weak-point. Viewers have criticised this scene for years saying it's ridiculous that a moon-sized battle station would have such a blatant weakness.

In Rogue One, it is explained that this weak-point was constructed intentionally by an engineer who was forced to work on the Death Star.

Although Rogue One seems to fix this plothole, it creates a totally new inconsistency. The film ends with the Rebels stealing the Death Star data and giving it to Princess Leia. The movie concludes with Darth Vader staring at Leia's blockade runner flying away.

The beginning of Star Wars takes place seconds after the ending of Rogue One. When Vader enters the blockade runner and confronts Leia, she denies having the Death Star plans. Vader should say, "Eh... I just saw the Rebels give you the plans. That is literally the worst lie ever."

189. Saw

Two men wake up to learn they have been kidnapped by a man called Jigsaw and he has trapped them in a room with a dead body. They are forced to find clues to learn why they have been abducted. In the end, we learn that the body on the floor is not really dead and is revealed to be Jigsaw himself.

Considering the two abductees are in this room for about seven hours, many viewers point out how ridiculous it is that Jigsaw managed not to show that he was breathing at any point.

But in Saw III, Jigsaw explains how he took a muscle relaxant just before he pretended to be dead to stop him from moving for several hours.

But there is a much bigger plothole – Why is Jigsaw in the room in the first place? If he needs a dead body (which he doesn't,) why doesn't Jigsaw get an actual dead body? His traps have killed several people so I'm sure he has one or two dead bodies to spare.

The only reason Jigsaw seems to be in the room is for the sake of a plot twist.

190. Saw II

To enjoy these movies, you have to ignore the obvious plothole – How can Jigsaw devise dozens of complex traps, kidnapped people, and make tape recordings while battling brain cancer?

And you know what? I can make my peace with that plothole. It's the entire premise of the franchise so I don't mind it.

But in this film, we learn that Jigsaw was in a car crash immediately after his diagnosis. And it wasn't a mild crash. He had jagged metal embedded into his flesh.

So not only did a man in his 60s get skewered by his car and develop terminal brain cancer, he had the strength to build 30 traps, each of which would require an absurd level of engineering? Did the brain tumour give him superpowers?

191. Saw III

Jeff's son was accidentally run over by a drunk driver called Timothy. Although the incident was witnessed by a passer-by called Danica, she didn't testify against Timothy and so, the judge only gave him six months in jail.

Jigsaw kidnaps Danica, the judge, and Timothy and places them in traps so Jeff can have his revenge against them.

However, since Danica didn't tell anyone about the incident, how did Jigsaw know about her?

192. Scream

While Sidney enters the bathroom at school, she learns that the serial killer, Ghostface is in one of the stalls. He jumps out of the stall and tries to attack Sidney but she manages to escape.

This means that Ghostface entered the girl's bathroom and stood on a toilet in a stall just to scare Sidney on the off-chance that she went to the bathroom.

How did nobody see Ghostface enter the bathroom? How did nobody see him leave, especially if Sydney reported the encounter? Also, why would Ghostface do this in broad daylight in a building with hundreds of witnesses?

This scene adds nothing to the plot or characters, which makes it more confusing.

193. Se7en
You can see Gluttony breathing despite the fact he's supposed to be dead. You can see Lust blinking despite being dead. How difficult is it for an actor to pretend to be dead? I assumed that would be pretty easy.

194. The Shawshank Redemption
Andy escapes his cell through a hole in the wall and then hides the hole with a poster.

How does he put the poster back up? The poster is secured on all four corners, which is impossible from inside the hole.

195. Shrek
When Princess Fiona asks Shrek and Donkey what Lord Farquad is like, they repeatedly mock his height.

However, there was no way the pair could have seen that Farquad was a dwarf when they met him.

196. Signs
The aliens in this film will die if they are exposed to water. Many people have pointed out that it's stupid for the aliens to invade Earth, considering 71% of the planet's surface is water.

What's even dumber is the fact that the aliens regularly walk through dew-covered cornfields throughout the film. If they are allergic to water, walking through these cornfields should kill them immediately.

197. The Simpsons Movie
The residents of Springfield are encased inside a colossal glass dome. The Simpsons escape to the other side of a dome through a hole. Not one person in Springfield attempts to escape the same way. Are there no shovels in Springfield?

198. Sinister
When Ethan Hawke's character, Ellison discovers a suspicious reel of film, he puts it in a projector

and turns it on to learn what's on it. The footage shows a man committing several murders.

One thing that is very strange about the footage (which is really common in films where a character finds a mysterious reel of film) is that it's edited. Obviously, the reel is edited to highlight the most interesting points for the viewer.

However, it doesn't make any sense in the context of the film. Did the killer film his murders and then think, "Ok, the first half of that murder was a little boring so I am going to edit it a bit so it'll be more interesting when someone stumbles upon this reel."

Also, you can't cut, edit, and stitch a film reel unless you have been trained. Did the killer take an editing course in-between murders?

199. The Sixth Sense

The story revolves around Haley Joel Osment's character, Cole being able to see dead people. Bruce Willis' character, Dr. Malcolm Crowe is tasked with helping Cole.

It is later revealed that Crowe was dead the whole time. This is considered to be the one of the greatest twists in movie history.

However, it falls apart when you ask the question – What kind of life was Crowe living where he didn't notice that no one was talking to him for several months apart from one child? If he went to Starbucks, would he find it odd that no one could hear or see him? Has he noticed that he hasn't eaten in weeks? Has Crowe ever thought, "Hey! I haven't been to the toilet in months!"

I know what you're thinking. Cole says that the ghosts "don't know they are dead." Okay. Maybe Crowe isn't aware of the passage of time. Maybe Crowe hasn't noticed that he hasn't paid rent in months and still hasn't been evicted.

So how did he find out about Cole? The first time you watch the film, you assume Cole's mother hired Crowe to treat her son. Now that we know that isn't true, how did Crowe become aware of the boy? Why did he walk into Cole's house in the first place if he wasn't invited?

200. Skyfall

James Bond tracks down the terrorist, Silva and has him captured. We learn that Silva wanted to be imprisoned so he could get closer to Bond's boss, M. Using a computer virus, Silva deactivates his cell door and escapes through the London Underground. Bond chases Silva and is about to shoot him but is stopped when the criminal blows up a tunnel, causing a train to come crashing through, which Bond narrowly dodges. Silva then escapes from the

Underground and heads to the court hearing that M is speaking at.

This is one of those plotholes that makes less sense the more you think about it. How did Silva know he had to detonate that tunnel unless he knew Bond would chase him to that position at that exact time? What if he mistimed it by five seconds, allowing Bond to kill him?

It was always Silva's plan to kill M during her court hearing. But how did Silva know M would be at the hearing at the same time as his incarceration?

Just to remind you, Silva didn't give himself up to MI6. He was captured. On the day he was imprisoned, Silva had no idea that MI6 had located him.

Silva's plan can't work because there are simply too many variables for him to control. This is quite a common plothole in stories where a villain intentionally allows himself to be incarcerated e.g. Khan in Star Trek: Into Darkness, Loki in The Avengers, the Joker in The Dark Knight, etc.

201. Sleeping Beauty

The wicked witch, Maleficent places a curse on Princess Aurora so she will fall into a death-like sleep when she pricks her finger on a spinning wheel on her 16th birthday. The king destroys all the spinning wheels in the kingdom and Aurora is hidden and protected by a trio of fairies, Flora, Fauna, and Merryweather.

Although the fairies are incredibly protective of Aurora throughout her life, they decide to take it easy, play around with magical spells, and leave Aurora alone on her 16th birthday. This means they guarded her every day except the one day she was meant to be guarded!

202. Snow White and the Seven Dwarfs
Why are all the dwarves poor if they mine diamonds?

203. The Sound of Music
The film concludes with the Von Trapps escaping the Nazis by making their way to Switzerland. However, the last scene shows the Von Trapps in Berchtesgaden, Obersalzburg… which is in Germany… which is a country that Nazis definitely live in.

204. Spider-Man
How come nobody can figure out that Peter Parker is Spider-Man? Dozens of his classmates saw him showcase superstrength and agility the same time that Spider-Man appears.

Also, the wrestling manager worked with Spider-Man. He saw Peter's unmasked face just before he got robbed.

Why is he keeping that information to himself? It's not like he owes Peter anything. In fact, Peter had the opportunity to stop the wrestling arena from being robbed and he didn't. Why doesn't that manager go to the cops and reveal Spider-Man's identity?

Also, how did Peter make the Spidersuit? Does he have super-sewing skills? You might think, 'Well, it's a comic book movie. How else can you explain it?'

In the comic, his Spidersuit was made by the wrestling company that Spider-Man worked for. That explanation makes way more sense.

205. Spider-Man 2

In the comics and films, Peter Parker usually has financial issues. In this film, his money problems are so severe, his aunt has to sell her house.

So why doesn't Peter work for the company, Oscorp? He is so intelligent that the company's founder, Norman Osborn was baffled that Peter could understand his theories.

Also, Peter's best friend, Harry Osborn is the CEO of Oscorp. Why doesn't Harry help him get a job? In fact, since Harry inherited billions from his father, why doesn't he just give a sum to Peter?

But that's not the only problem with this movie. A scientist called Otto Octavius performs a science experiment using four metallic tentacles that are fused into his spine. He intends to use his apparatus to harness a dangerous and unpredictable energy source called tridium.

The experiment fails, which leads to the death of Octavius' wife. Octavius goes insane and becomes the supervillain, Doctor Octopus

Nobody points out one really important fact - Octavius has cured paralysis. Octavius can control his tentacles telepathically, since they are linked to his brain. Why doesn't he use that technology to make billions rather than using it to tap into an energy source that is so dangerous, it can destroy the entire city?

206. Spider-Man 3

Harry Osborn is obsessed with Spider-Man, believing the superhero is responsible for killing his father, Norman.

At the end of the film, his butler tells Harry that Norman accidentally killed himself. Why the butler waited this long to tell Harry the truth is never explained. Although this is the plothole that people criticise the most, there is another one that irks me more.

The symbiote, Venom happens to land on Earth less than 100ft away from the world's biggest superhero. What are the odds of that?

207. Spider-Man: Homecoming

In the previous Marvel film, Captain America: Civil War, Tony Stark emphasises that superheroes have to take responsibility for the collateral damage caused by their actions. That was literally the entire premise of that film.

But in Spider-Man: Homecoming, Tony Stark gives a 15-year-old a Spidersuit with an Instant-Kill-Mode. Then Tony Stark has the gall to say that Spider-Man is irresponsible.

But that's not the only plothole in this film. Although the Spidersuit has a tracker, Peter Parker's friend, Ned removes it. Just to remind you, Tony Stark is probably the fourth or fifth smartest person in the world. And yet, a teenager was able to hack Tony's hardware.

208. Split

Kevin Wendell Crumb is a kidnapper who suffers Disassociate Identity Disorder, causing him to develop 24 personalities.

Just before he kills his counsellor, she writes down his real name, knowing that Kevin will revert to normal if it is said aloud.

The girl that Kevin abducts, Casey finds the counsellor's note and cries out Kevin's name, returning him to his original personality.

However, if the counsellor knew saying Kevin's name would revert him to normal, why didn't she say it herself?

209.   Star Trek: The Motion Picture
The crew of the Starship Enterprise discover a living machine called V'Ger, which seems to destroy everything in its path. The crew later learn that V'Ger is Voyager 6; an Earth satellite from the 20th century which has been lost for centuries. It's called V'Ger because the "oya" and "6" in its name was covered in dirt when it was rediscovered.

However, why would the satellite call itself V'Ger? It's still programmed as Voyager 6 so why would it refer to itself as anything else?

This would be like if you covered the letter "m" on a MacBook, causing the computer to refer to itself as an AcBook on the loading screen.

210.   Star Trek II: The Wrath of Khan
The USS Reliant seeks out a planet with no life so they can test their Genesis device; a machine that can terraform a dead world so it can harbour life. The ship has great difficulty finding a world that has no life despite the fact that every planet in

our Solar System can't sustain life apart from Earth. Why don't they just go to our Solar System and test Genesis on Mars, Venus, or Mercury?

211. Star Trek

After being marooned on an ice planet, Captain Kirk finds shelter in a cave where he bump into Spock who has been stranded there for years. Kirk was only on the planet for about ten minutes before stumbling into Spock.

Okay, let's break this down. Imagine there was one human being on Earth. Now imagine that an alien lands on the planet. Despite the fact that the planet is nearly 25,000 miles in equatorial circumference, the alien happens to land ten minutes away from the only human in the world. What are the odds of that?

Also, Spock is marooned on the planet with Scotty, who happens to know how to teleport Kirk back to his ship. That's like if a coincidence took steroids.

212. Star Trek: Into Darkness

Khan is one of 73 superhumans; each containing regenerating blood that is so advanced, it can reanimate the dead.

After Captain Kirk sacrifices himself to realign the warp core of his ship, Spock desperately hunts down Khan to take a sample of his blood to revive Kirk.

Why doesn't Spock use the blood from the other 72 superhumans?

Despite the fact this blood has basically cured death, it is never mentioned or used in the sequel.

213. Star Wars: Episode I – The Phantom Menace

The opening text states that Obi-Wan is a Jedi Knight. A droid confirms this in the first scene. In the final scene, it is announced that Obi-Wan has finally become a Jedi Knight.

While Obi-Wan and his master, Qui-Gon's fight an army of droids, they escape using Force Speed. This power is never used again for the rest of the franchise. That power would have come in really handy in the final battle.

214. Star Wars: Episode II – Attack of the Clones

The assassin, Zam attempts to kill Queen Amidala by sending a drone to her bedroom window. The drone cuts the glass of her window and spews out two toxic worms to poison her.

Why didn't the assassin just get the drone to shoot her?

Also, if the Jedi knew an assassin was trying to assassinate Amidala, why place her in a room with a window?

215. Star Wars: Episode III – Revenge of the Sith

Amidala dies moments after she gives birth to Luke and Leia. But in Return of the Jedi, Leia tells Luke that she remembers her mother. How? Leia was about ten seconds old when Amidala died.

216. Star Wars: Episode IV - A New Hope

In the opening scene Leia inserts the plans for the Death Star in the droid, R2-D2. R2-D2 and his companion, C-3P0 then enter an escape pod, which blasts into space.

Although the Empire's Star Destroyer has an opportunity to destroy the escape pod, the commander refuses, since their scanners show that the pod contains no lifeforms.

Considering the Star Destroyer has a bajillion laser guns, I'm pretty sure the Empire can shoot the pod. There is literally no disadvantage at shooting at it.

217. Star Wars: Episode V – The Empire Strikes Back

Yoda trains Luke Skywalker how to use the Force while Han Solo and Leia are being chased by the

Empire. When Han and Leia are captured, Luke finishes his training and goes to rescue them.

The continuity of these events doesn't match up. Was Han and Leia being chased for months or did Luke learn how to use the Force in a day or two?

In the prequels, Jedis take years to master the ways of the Force. Some would argue this point by saying the "prequels don't count" ... which is true.

218. Star Wars: Episode VI – Return of the Jedi

Luke Skywalker's plan to retrieve Han Solo from Jabba the Hutt's palace is completely nonsensical. He sends C-3PO and R2-D2 to the palace as a gift to Jabba in exchange for Han (unbeknownst to them.) Jabba refuses to bargain but keeps the droids.

Leia then enters the palace disguised as a bounty hunter called Boushh.

Wait, why send Leia to infiltrate the palace when Lando already did? Why didn't Lando do anything?

Anyway, when Leia believes Jabba is asleep, she attempts to rescue Han. Jabba reveals himself and captures them both.

Shortly after, Luke shows up and has an epic showdown with Jabba's forces, killing them, and rescuing his friends.

This plan falls apart from the very beginning. What if Jabba agreed to trade Han for the droids? If he did that, Luke would still have to rescue the droids.

Why did Luke send the droids in the first place if Leia was going to attempt to rescue Han shortly after? You can argue that the reason the droids were sent is because R2-D2 was loaded with Luke's lightsabre, which he launches at Luke when he battles Jabba's forces at the Sarlaac Pit.

But how did Luke know he was going to be taken to the Sarlaac Pit? Even if Jabba has a reputation for sending his prisoners there, this plan falls apart (again) if Jabba kept the droids or if Leia successfully rescued Han.

219. Star Wars: The Force Awakens

To show the power of the Starkiller Base, General Hux fires its laser at the Hosnian quadrant, wiping out the entire star system.

So, how long do you think it would take for that laser to reach every planet in that star system?

Well, if the laser is firing at the speed of light, it will take... about four years. It takes eight minutes for the Sun's light to reach Earth and five-and-a-half hours for it to reach Pluto.

The Starkiller Base has to be in the neighbouring system to siphon the power of the nearest star. Since a star is about four light years away (at the very closest,) it would take four years for the laser to reach every planet in the Hosnian system. This means that Hux was firing that laser non-stop for about 1,460 days, which is obviously impossible since we see the Hosnian system being destroyed after a few minutes.

What I'm trying to say is that this Star Wars film isn't scientifically accurate.

220. Star Wars: The Last Jedi

Throughout the film, The First Order's vessel, The Dreadnought pursues The Resistance's ship. After the ship is evacuated, The Resistance's Vice Admiral, Holdo turns the ship around and rams into The Dreadnought at lightspeed, shredding both ships. This concept bothered a lot of viewers as Holdo refused to divulge this plan to her crew for seemingly no reason.

However, there's a much, much bigger problem with Holdo's decision. This is the first time in any Star Wars film where a character has used their ship, for a lack of a better word, as a bullet by smashing it into a target at lightspeed.

Why has no one ever done this before? Although the X-Wings are tiny, they will cause irreparable damage if they smashed into any structure at lightspeed. How come no one did that to the three Death Stars in the previous movies?

But it gets worse. The Empire's Death Star is a battle station that is capable of destroying an entire planet. Why did they build such a gargantuan weapon when all they have to do to destroy a planet is make one of their ships collide into one at lightspeed?

It doesn't matter how big the ship is. If a solid object collides with a planet at lightspeed, it's going to smash right through it. This is the worst kind of plothole because it creates plotholes in other movies in the franchise.

221. Starship Troopers
Carl explains that the Bugs can be killed by shooting at their nerve stem. He demonstrates this and kills a Bug instantly.

Every soldier dismisses this and shoots the Bugs randomly, wasting countless bullets.

222. Suicide Squad
When Harley Quinn leaves the Suicide Squad for the Joker, Amanda Waller orders Rick Flag to activate the bomb in her neck.

Since the Joker deactivated the bomb, it doesn't work. However, there's nothing stopping Flag from shooting her in the head.

223. Superman

Lex Luthor launches two missiles on opposite sides of the United States, believing that Superman can't stop them both from detonating. It turns out that Lex is right as Superman stops one missile, allowing the other to detonate, causing untold destruction.

Luckily, Superman flies at the speed of light, turning back time, which allows him to stop the other missile.

However, if Superman can fly at the speed of light (186,000 miles per second,) how come he can't travel from one side of the US to the other in a few minutes, which is only 2,800 miles wide? That should take Superman 0.02 seconds! And yet, he couldn't catch both missiles in two minutes?

224. Superman II

When Lois Lane learns that Clark Kent is Superman, he decides to give up his power to be with her. He goes to The Fortress of Solitude in the North Pole and exposes himself to Red Kryptonite, leaving him powerless. In the next scene, Clark and Lois are back in the US. How did they get back to America from the North Pole?

225. Superman III
Richard Pryor's character, Gus, earns $85,000 by stealing half a cent from each employee. This means that his company has... 17 million employees.

By comparison, Apple had 132,000 fulltime employees in 2018.

226. Superman IV: The Quest for Peace
In the final battle, Lois Lane breathes in space. This might be the dumbest plothole in movie history.

227. Superman Returns
When a Sunstone is exposed to water, it transforms into a huge crystal. One of these Sunstones formed The Fortress of Solitude that Superman lives in.

Lex Luthor inserts Kryptonite into a Sunstone before dunking it into the ocean, which turns it into a continent. Since Superman is vulnerable to Kryptonite, he is completely powerless on this land mass.

Despite this, he lifts the entire structure up from underneath and then hurls it into space.

228. Tangled

The villain, Gothel has maintained her youth for centuries by singing a special song to a magical flower.

How did Gothel find out what to sing to the flower to make this spell work? Did Gothel try every song possible until one of them made her young? How did she know singing would make it work? WHY does singing work? How did she know the flower had the power to grant eternal youth?

229. Tarzan

If Tarzan has been living in the Jungle for years, why doesn't he have a beard?

230. Teenage Mutant Ninja Turtles

To avoid being publicly exposed, the ninja turtles wear disguises when they are out in the open. What's their disguise? A trench coat and a fedora. How does that fool everyone?

Also, you might be think the turtles only venture out like this when it is necessary.

Nope. Raphael dresses like this to go to the movie theatre to watch Critters. So Raphael bought a ticket and sat in a room with hundreds of people and NOBODY thought he looked suspicious? Could Raphael have at least watched a good film like Citizen Kane or something?

231. Teenage Mutant Ninja Turtles II: Secret of the Ooze

When the Shredder is exposed to the ooze, it mutates him into the Super Shredder, making him far taller, stronger, and more muscular.

The ooze also gives his armour more spikes. How does that work?

232. Teenage Mutant Ninja Turtles (2014)

The villain, Eric Sachs drives the turtles from New York City to his mansion on the snowy mountain in...wait... there are no snowy mountains near New York! The director could have avoided this plothole by looking at a map.

Also, Sach's evil plan makes no sense. Sachs intends to poison the city so he can save the people with mutagen, which can regenerate any organism on a cellular level. The big question is – Why doesn't he just... sell the mutagen anyway? It's the biggest medical breakthrough in history! That's like if Sachs discovered the cure for cancer but instead of selling it, he gave everyone in the world cancer then cured them just to prove his cure worked.

And what is Sachs' motivation? To be mega-rich. Those are his exact words. So, a rich entrepreneur poisons millions of people to be... richer?

I know the story that revolves around ninja turtles wouldn't make sense but could the writers try a little bit?

233. Teenage Mutant Ninja Turtles: Out of the Shadows

I can't believe this story makes LESS sense than the cartoon and the comics that inspired this film. In the animated series, mutagen causes a human's DNA to merge with the last animal they touched. Because Bebop touched a warthog before being exposed to mutagen, he turns into a boar/human hybrid. Since Rocksteady touched a rhinoceros before being exposed to mutagen, he turned into a rhino/human hybrid.

Although this film could have copied this concept, the scientist, Baxter tells Shredder that Bebop and Rocksteady turn into these hybrids when exposed to mutagen because humans share DNA with warthogs and rhinos……. No they don't! Says who? No evolutionist has ever believed that!

234. The Terminator

In the future, a machine called Skynet becomes sentient and launches all of Earth's nuclear missiles upon humanity, killing three billion people. A man called John Connor forms a resistance force against the machines and emerges victorious.

The surviving robots use a time-machine to send a Terminator back in time to kill John Connor's mother before John is born. If John was never born, he will never have formed the resistance force, meaning that Skynet will easily destroy all of humanity.

Although the Terminator is defeated, Skynet just sends another one. And another one. And another one. This plot has the same problem as most time-travel films (as I have already explained when I discussed Back to the Future II.) Skynet can send an infinite amount of Terminators back through time. Even if one of the Terminators succeed in killing John Connor, the resistance can send one of their fighters back to stop John from getting killed.

So, what's the easiest way to win the war against Skynet once and for all?

Simple. Find out who invented the time machine and kill him.

235. Terminator 2: Judgment Day

In The Terminator, Kyle Reese explains that he couldn't time-travel with weapons because "nothing dead can go through the time-machine." The Terminators can time-travel because their skeleton is covered in real skin and blood.

This concept is thrown out the window since the villain, the T-1000 can use the time machine despite being made of liquid metal.

236. Terminator 3: Rise of the Machines
Sometimes, a plothole doesn't become a plothole until it is acknowledged. In this film, a bunch of people try to lift the Terminator but they can't since he "weighs a ton."

If the Terminator weighs so much, how can he hold onto a crane without weighing it down? How can he drive a car if he weighs more than the vehicle? I never thought of that until I heard that line in this film. Now that's all I can think about when I watch the title character drive in the first two films. Damn you, Terminator 3! You can ruin anything!

237. Terminator: Salvation
How can Marcus not realise he is a Terminator if he sees everything in infrared? Last time I checked, humans don't see like that.

238. Terminator: Genisys
Why does Kyle Reese and Sarah Connor time-travel days before Skynet takes over the world? Why would they force themselves to try and destroy Skynet with so little time? Why don't

they go back several months or years to ensure Skynet never comes to be?

239. The Thing

A group of Antarctic explorers discover there is a shapeshifting alien among them. The primary weapon that the explorers use to defeat the alien is a flamethrower.

There is never any explanation why the explorers are equipped with such a device. If you think explorers have them to unthaw sensitive material, a flamethrower is the worst tool to possibly use. It's incredibly heavy, unpredictable, and empties its fuel within a few seconds.

240. Thor

After Thor declares war against the Frost Giant without his father's consent, he is banished from his home of Asgard and is sent to Earth.

However, Thor only attacked the Frost Giants because he was goaded by his manipulative stepbrother, Loki. Now that Thor is out of the way, Loki is the only successor for the throne of Asgard.

But Loki wants to prove his worth to his father, so he declares war on the Frost Giants. So… Loki thinks he will make Odin proud by carrying out the same action as Thor which is what made his father banished him from Asgard. If Loki did nothing, he would still be the successor of Asgard.

241. Thor: The Dark World

The villain, Malekith the Accursed attempts to destroy the universe because... reasons. With only seconds before he achieves his plan, Thor manages to kill Malekith.

If Malekith was that dangerous, why didn't the Avengers team up to stop him? The entire universe is in jeopardy and they think they should just leave it to Thor?

They teamed up in Avengers: Age of Ultron because they suspected a terrorist group was weaponizing alien tech. They teamed up for that but not when the universe nearly exploded?

242. Thor: Ragnarok

Thor is the God of Thunder, allowing him to control and shoot lightning. Throughout the film, The Grand Master and Valkyrie regularly knock Thor out... with electricity. Of everything they could have used to subdue him, they chose the one thing he can control. That's like defeating the god of the sea, Poseidon with water.

243. Thunderball

In most James Bond films, Q gives Bond a series of weapons, which are disguised as innocuous items. When they meet, Q gives Bond a Geiger counter, which is disguised as a watch.

However, Bond later refers to his camera as the Geiger counter.

244. Titanic

After the ship sinks, Rose avoids freezing to death in the icy cold ocean by lying on a floating door. Her lover, Jack refuses to lay on the door with her and so, freezes to death.

Although many people criticise this scene because there was plenty of room on the door for Jack, I never had a problem with this scene. Although there was enough space for both of them, it may have toppled over due to Jack's extra weight.

Even if it didn't, Jack didn't want to risk it and so, he let Rose lay on the door to guarantee that at least one of them would survive the night.

What I did have a problem with is the fact that Rose tells this whole story in flashback and yet, is able to recount events effortlessly from over 80 years ago… that she didn't even witness! Rose discusses her time on the Titanic to the treasure hunter, Brock Lovett. How does she tell Brock about the events that occurred to Jack before he boarded the Titanic if she wasn't there?

245. Top Gun

The ending revolves around Top Gun pilot, Maverick battling six enemy fighter jets from North Korea. After rescuing a communications ship, Maverick destroys four enemy jets and returns to base.

Although this is supposed to be a happy ending, the implied aftermath is catastrophic. Maverick invaded another country in a fighter jet and killed four pilots.

In case you didn't know, you're not allowed to do that. Although the film ends without Maverick suffering any consequences, his actions would have initiated World War III between North Korea and the United States.

However, I will forgive this film for this plothole since it has the best theme song ever.

246. Toy Story

If Buzz Lightyear keeps insisting that he's not a toy, why does he freeze like the other toys anytime humans walk by?

247. Toy Story 2

Although Al gets on a plane to Japan, he is seen on TV in America the very next day. How is that possible? It would take about ten hours to reach Japan. How could he go to Japan and back in such a short time?

248. Toy Story 3
If SunnySide is filmed 24/7, how come security workers have never seen the toys moving around?

249. Transformers: The Movie
Many Transformers in this film die including Prowl, Ironhide, Brawn, and Ratchet. The Autobot leader, Optimus Prime is fatally injured when the Decepticon leader, Megatron stabs him. He dies shortly after.

However, when Ultra Magnus is blown up later, the Autobots easily resurrect him by simply putting him back together. If the Autobots can fix Ultra Magnus so easily, why don't they do the same for the other deceased Transformers?

Also, why is Optimus Prime's death such a big deal? He died over 25 times in the animated series (including in the first episode.) If they have resurrected Prime over two dozen times before, why are the Autobots not trying to resuscitate him this time?

250. Transformers
Megatron desperately seeks out the Allspark; a device that can make any technology become sentient. Despite the fact the Allspark's purpose

is to create life, it ends up killing Megatron. How? It's never explained.

But don't worry. Megatron is resurrected in the sequel. How? With the Allspark. This is means that Megatron was killed and resurrected with the exact same thing. That's like shooting someone dead and then shooting them back to life.

251. Transformers: Revenge of the Fallen
Despite the fact that the Decepticons attacked a city in the previous film, the world's government managed to hide the existence of the Transformers from society.

This is impossible since thousands of people witnessed the Autobots and Decepticons fighting in Mission City near Vancouver. Are you telling me not one person in the city recorded the battle on their phone?

252. Transformers: Dark of the Moon
Sentinel Prime creates a wormhole so the Transformers' world of Cybertron can teleport through. Sentinel Prime can then use the resources of Earth to reactivate his planet.

In the middle of this teleportation, the machine that controls the wormhole turns off. Sentinel Prime turns it back on moments shortly after.

Since the wormhole stopped while Cybertron was passing through it, the planet should be cut in half. However, when the wormhole is turned back on, the planet is perfectly intact.

253. Transformers: Age of Extinction

Most of Chicago was destroyed in the events that occurred in the previous film. In one of the first scenes of this film, we see a sign that reads "REMEMBER CHICAGO."

However, when the characters go to Chicago, the whole city has been rebuilt. How do you rebuild an entire city in five years? It takes longer to rebuild one skyscraper!

254. Transformers: The Last Knight

Quintessa intends to bring the Transformers' homeworld of Cybertron to Earth... despite the fact that Cybertron was completely destroyed two movies ago. How did the director forget that? Does he watch his own movies?

Also, when Bumblebee speaks in the final scene, Optimus Prime points out that this is the first time he has heard his ally's voice since they lived on Cybertron.

This isn't true since Optimus hears Bumblebee speak in the events that took place in the first Transformers movie.

255. Twilight

In the Twilight movies, vampires sparkle when they are exposed to sunlight. Throughout every film, there are scenes where vampires (usually Edward) are clearly in sunlight and yet, they are not sparkling.

256. Twilight: New Moon

Although Edward is a vampire, he has fallen in love with a mortal called Bella. Sadly, Edward decides he can't be with her because he doesn't want to put Bella in danger.

When Edward believes that Bella has committed suicide, he snaps and decides to reveal the existence of vampires to the public.

Before Edward makes this decision, couldn't he have doublechecked to see if Bella is alive? Facebook? Twitter? Phone call?

But it doesn't end there. In this story, vampires have superspeed so I'll assume he could have reached her house in a day or two at most.

Also, Edward's friend is telepathic. Why doesn't she just scan the minds of Bella's friends and family to see if she is alive or not?

257. Twister

The story revolves around a group of meteorologists chasing down a series of tornados. From the very beginning, the film emphasises that an F5 is the most powerful type of tornado. If somebody says "F5," everyone in the room stops talking out of fear. An F5 creates winds from 261-318mph that can uplift trees, hurl cars like missiles, topple skyscrapers, and rip houses from their foundations. Since this is a movie, we know the protagonists are going to survive the F5.

How? By tying themselves to a pipe with a belt. Somehow, this 300+mph twister doesn't uproot the pipe, rip the belt, or pull the limbs off the main characters.

Also, there's a scene where the tornado roars. Tornados can't do that.

258. The Usual Suspects

A man called Verbal Kint is interrogated by Agent Kujan after he is the only person to witness the events on San Pedro Bay that led to the murder of 27 people.

At the end of the film, Kujan learns that Kint lied throughout his entire interrogation, piecing together details for his story from the bulletin board behind the agent.

All Kujan had to do to learn that Kint was lying is face the direction of the bulletin board for a couple of seconds. Why didn't Kint have a lie prepared?

259. V for Vendetta

The story takes place in a totalitarian Britain. In the beginning, Evey heads out to meet her friend, Dietrich. She is stopped by Fingermen police who remind her that she is out at 11pm and curfew is 1030.

The Fingermen begin to assault Evey but she is rescued by a masked man called V, who intends to destroy the government's rule.

When she decided to meet Dietrich, how did that conversation go?

Dietrich: Okay, Evey, I'll see you at 11.
Evey: Isn't that past curfew?
Dietrich: Yeah, but it will be fine.
Evey: You do know if I'm caught by the police, I'll be arrested or killed?
Dietrich: Yeah, pretty much.
Evey: I see you first thing in the morning, right? Can't we just talk then?
Dietrich: Nah.
Evey: Why don't we just meet BEFORE curfew... you know... when it's not illegal.
Dietrich: Yeah, I'm not feeling it.
Evey: Okay, see you then.

Basically, this whole "breaking curfew" scene was created to give Evey an excuse to bump into V even though it doesn't make any sense.

260. Venom

Riot is an alien symbiote who needs to move from host to host to survive. However, Riot manages to survive in an elderly woman for six months. How is that possible?

Even the director admitted that he couldn't figure out how to get around this. In his own words, "That's one of our logic bumps. We had to have a passage of time in order to show Eddie's downfall, and that was the one thing that doesn't entirely track."

261. The Village

The story seems to revolve around a 18th century American colony that live in an enclosed village. The inhabitants never leave the village because they are told that monsters reside in the forest.

We later learn that the story takes place in the 21st century and the "monsters" were made up to hide the fact the village is cut off from the modern world.

How come no hikers, hunters, or passer-bys have ever stumbled upon the village?

I know what you're thinking. It's a movie so you have to suspend your disbelief to enjoy the story.

However, the village resides in Pennsylvania, which has a population of over 12 million. It is the fifth most populated state in the United

States. If this story took place in a remote area in Canada, this plothole could be easily avoided.

262. WALL-E

In the future, Earth has become an inhospitable wasteland, forcing humanity to leave the planet and live on a colossal spaceship called the Axiom. A robot called EVA is sent to Earth for recon and learns that life is beginning to thrive again. She returns to the Axiom to tell the captain that they can now return to Earth.

However, the ship's AI, Auto has secret orders not to return to Earth… so why was EVA sent to Earth in the first place? Why would Auto initiate the one action that could jeopardise his protocol?

263. The Wizard of Oz

When the Scarecrow is given an honorary diploma, he says, "The sum of the square roots of any two sides of an isosceles triangle is equal to the square root of the remaining side."

That is not true. So, in an attempt to make the Scarecrow look smart, the writers made him look like an idiot.

264. The Wolverine

The film begins by showing a flashback of Wolverine saving an officer called Yashida from the atomic blast of Nagasaki during World War II.

The story skips 64 years into the future where Wolverine meets a girl called Yukio who says he must come to Japan with her to meet Yashida who is now dying of old age.

He remembers Yashida despite the fact that it has been mentioned in every single X-Men film that Wolverine suffers amnesia so he can't remember anything about his past.

265.   Wreck-It Ralph

Ralph is a video game character in the game, Fix-It Felix Jr. Felix is seen as a hero since he has the ability to fix anything with his hammer. Ralph is sick and tired of being depicted as a villain and escapes from his game and goes on an adventure with another video game character called Vanellope.

Like Ralph, Vanellope feels like she doesn't fit in because she causes glitches in her game. Throughout the film, Ralph tries to help Vanellope, worried that she might get erased from her game.

However, if Felix just taps Vanellope with his hammer, it should stop her glitching immediately. Despite the fact we see Felix fix tons of things throughout the story, nobody considers this.

Also, why is the Street Fighter character, Zangief, in The Bad Guy Meeting when he is a hero in his game? Street Fighter is one of the most famous games ever. How did the director not know that?

266. X-Men

Professor Charles Xavier has the ability to control people's minds if he is in their proximity. However, he can't do this to his enemy, Magneto because he wears a special helmet that renders him immune to psychic attacks.

So why doesn't Xavier use Cerebro to find Magneto's minions, Sabretooth, Toad, and Mystique? In one scene, the professor uses his powers to control Sabretooth to grab Magneto by the neck. What does Xavier do after that?

He lets Magneto go. He could have used his powers to make Sabretooth take off Magneto's helmet, allowing Xavier to put Magneto into a coma.

267. X2: X-Men 2 United

Charles Xavier uses his psychic powers to freeze everyone in a room after his student, Pyro reveals his mutant powers. Xavier then wipes everyone's memory of the incident.

If Xavier has the ability to freeze everyone in his proximity with little effort, why doesn't he do this all the time? There are so many times throughout the franchise where Xavier could have stopped a villain by freezing them with his mind but didn't.

268. X-Men: The Last Stand

In the previous film, Magneto attempted to kill every human being on Earth. In the conclusion of this film, Magneto is depowered (kind of.)

Despite the fact that he has killed many people and is directly responsible for performing multiple terrorist attacks, Magneto is not incarcerated. The last scene shows him playing chess in a public park.

You might think that he hasn't been arrested simply because no one has recognized him. Not only is Magneto not wearing a disguise, he is playing chess in the Exact Same City he terrorised the day before!

269. X-Men Origins: Wolverine

Logan agrees to take part in the Weapon X program. During the procedure, his skeleton will be bonded with the indestructible metal, adamantium, making him almost unkillable. Because Logan is a mutant with the ability to heal from almost anything, he is the only person who can survive the experiment.

However, he doesn't know that the facilitator of Weapon X, William Stryker intends to erase Logan's memory and use him for his own evil schemes.

However, Stryker decides to erase Logan's memory AFTER he is made unkillable. Where's the logic in that?

Later, Stryker arms himself with a gun loaded with adamantium bullets and prepares to confront Logan. When one of his employees points out that Logan will heal from any gunshot wound, Stryker says, "His brain may heal but his memories won't grow back."

How the hell does he know that? Is he going to shoot Logan in the memory part of his brain and miss every other part? The brain doesn't work like that!

270. X-Men: First Class

In the conclusion, Charles Xavier is paralysed by a stray bullet. Although Xavier is in his 20s, he was seen walking in X-Men: The Last Stand when he is in his 40s or 50s.

Now, you could argue that this story takes place in an alternative timeline. However, this film has the exact same beginning as the original X-Men film to confirm that this take places in the same timeline.

Speaking of which, Xavier told Wolverine in X-Men that Magneto helped build Cerebro.

We see in this film that Cerebro was built by Hank McCoy. This plothole could have been fixed if we saw Magneto assist with Cerebro's construction in anyway e.g. flip a switch, pull a lever, use his magnetism powers to lift machinery, etc.

271. X-Men: Days of Future Past

At the beginning of this book, you may have noticed that I gave this film a "Special Thanks." In fact, it was this film that inspired me to write this book. Despite the fact that X-Men: Days of Future Past is considered to be the best film in the franchise… it… doesn't… make… sense.

A scientist called Bolivar Trask constructs robots called Sentinels to hunt down mutants. To stop the beginning of a mutant war, Mystique shot Bolivar Trask dead.

Since Mystique has the ability to shapeshift, scientists captured her and used her shapeshifting abilities to create the adaptive Sentinels to wipe out mutantkind.

The opening scene takes place in the future where most mutants have been exterminated by the Sentinels. A mutant called Kitty Pryde uses her time-travelling powers to send Wolverine's consciousness back to 1973 to stop Mystique from killing Bolivar Trask.

Okay, that's the story. Now, let's look at the plotholes. If Mystique was captured and killed in 1973, how did she encounter the X-Men in the events that unfolded in the original trilogy, which took place in the 2000s?

Also, Bolivar Trask is a white dwarf in this film but he was normal-sized black man in X-Men: The Last Stand.

On top of that, Professor X was vaporized in that movie. How is he back to life in this film?

Now, I know there is a post-credits scene in X-Men: The Last Stand that shows the professor transferring his consciousness to another man at the last second.

Unless that other man is the professor's twin brother who he never mentioned (that is also paralysed,) this doesn't make any sense.

I know what you're thinking. It's obviously an alternative timeline, right? But the characters repeatedly remind the audience that this IS the same universe as the one we are familiar with. When Logan asks how the professor survived... exploding, the professor says, "As I told you a long time ago, Logan. You are not the only one with gifts." This is a direct reference to the first film, proving this story occurs in the same timeline.

Also, Kitty Pryde has appeared in three movies and has always been known for her ability to past through solid matter.

Her time-travel abilities were never mentioned and was only invented for the plot. This would be like if we suddenly found out that Wolverine can fly.

But you can dismiss that by saying time-travel is always messy in films. But there's a lot of simple flaws in the story that don't revolve around time-travel. The Sentinels can adapt to their surroundings since they are made of Mystique's shape-shifting cells. When the Sentinels fight Iceman, they can turn into fire. When they are being punched, the robots can turn into diamond. However, the mutant, Rogue has adaptive powers, not Mystique. All Mystique can do is change her appearance. She can't turn into fire or ice or diamond. Sorry, writers. You picked the wrong mutant.

Despite the fact that Mystique is repeatedly told that her actions will cause the death of every mutant, she refuses to listen to anyone. What's the point of trying to save mutants if your actions cause the death of all mutants?

Quicksilver can move at superspeed so the X-Men use his skills to break Magneto out of prison to help them.

After Magneto is freed, Quicksilver stops helping the X-Men... for no reason. Quicksilver is not used to help fight the Sentinels, stop Mystique from assassinating Trask, or preventing Magneto from dropping a baseball stadium around the US president, Richard Nixon. Despite the fact that the X-Men need all the help they can get, they don't ask Quicksilver to assist them even though the world as we know it will end if they fail.

The only thing Quicksilver did is rescue the guy... who tried to kill the president! If the X-Men didn't ask for Quicksilver's help, things would have gone a lot more smoothly.

At the end of the film, Wolverine is picked up by Stryker so he can be initiated into the Weapon X program. Stryker's eyes flash yellow, proving that he is actually Mystique in disguise. This is not addressed in the sequel, X-Men: Apocalypse as Logan is first seen in that film in the Weapon X program.

The final plothole is the one that bothers me the most. Although Charles Xavier is paralysed, he is able to walk by taking a concoction created by Hank McCoy. This poses a problem for the X-Men since the concoction's side effect causes Xavier to temporarily lose his mutant powers.

At no point in the entire series does anyone point out that Hank McCoy has CURED

PARALYSIS!! That's a pretty big deal! Why hasn't he won all the Nobel prizes?

www.ingramcontent.com/pod-product-compliance
Lightning Source LLC
Chambersburg PA
CBHW061948070426
42450CB00007BA/1094